Prisoners and Escape

Prisoners and Escape

Those Who Were There

Edited by

Rachel Bilton

Pen & Sword
MILITARY

First published in Great Britain in 2017 by
PEN & SWORD MILITARY
an imprint of
Pen & Sword Books Ltd
47 Church Street
Barnsley
South Yorkshire
S70 2AS

Copyright © Rachel Bilton, 2017

ISBN 978-1-47386-709-3

Typeset by Concept, Huddersfield, West Yorkshire, HD4 5JL.
Printed and bound in England by CPI Group (UK) Ltd, Croydon CR0 4YY.

Pen & Sword Books Ltd incorporates the imprints of Pen & Sword Archaeology, Atlas, Aviation, Battleground, Discovery, Family History, History, Maritime, Military, Naval, Politics, Railways, Select, Social History, Transport, True Crime, and Claymore Press, Frontline Books, Leo Cooper, Praetorian Press, Remember When, Seaforth Publishing and Wharncliffe.

For a complete list of Pen & Sword titles please contact
PEN & SWORD BOOKS LIMITED
47 Church Street, Barnsley, South Yorkshire, S70 2AS, England
E-mail: enquiries@pen-and-sword.co.uk
Website: www.pen-and-sword.co.uk

CONTENTS

LIST OF PLATES

Newly captured British troops headed by an officer are being escorted back from the fighting.

A group of prisoners with their unarmed guard who is obviously not expecting any problem from them.

An injured airman being helped from the crash site.

Prisoners watched by two guards and a group of onlookers leaving them little chance of escape.

Prisoners waiting to be processed behind the barbed wire of their new home.

Prisoners enter the inner camp through more gates and wire.

A perimeter watchtower.

Officers' quarters.

Guards patrolling the outer fence.

Other ranks' barracks.

These are the arms of Ruhleben Internment Camp in Berlin where most British male civilians were held.

A group of healthy and relatively young prisoners.

Officers' accommodation.

An officer's bedroom.

A failed escape tunnel that came to the surface too early.

A rope ladder down to the excavation of a tunnel hidden in a disused building.

Tools confiscated by guards.

Escapers all, recaptured officers in a room at Holzminden.

The escape tunnel at Holzminden after its discovery.

A compass discovered during an inspection of food parcels.

A parcel wrapped in a specific way.

The typical contents of a parcel.

A static guard is talking to a mounted guard who rode along the frontier.

The warning on the high tension wire between Belgium and Holland.

Officers looking at a Belgian who was electrocuted trying to get to Holland.

German guards using an insulated hook to remove a cat that touched the wire.

Harry Beaumont.

Hugh Durnford taken in 1918 at Stralsund Camp from where he escaped.

Duncan Grinnell-Milne.

A.J. Evans of the escaping club.

THE AUTHORS

Harry Beaumont
No biographical information available.

Wallace Ellison
When the war was declared, Ellison was a lecturer in Economics at Frankfurt University. He was arrested in August 1914 and held at Sennelager Camp. Shortly after being released, he was imprisoned again, this time at Ruhleben, from November 1914. After attempting escape he was moved to Stadtvogtei Prison, where he attempted escape again and was consequently moved back to Ruhleben from where he successfully escaped to Holland in October 1917. Until the end of the war he operated as a secret agent on the German-Swiss border.

A.J. Evans
Evans joined Inns of Court OTC on 5 August 1914. He was transferred to the Intelligence Corps, crossed to France in late August 1914 as temporary 2nd lieutenant and took part in the retreat. In February 1915, he joined the Royal Flying Corps, serving as an observer in No. 3 Squadron until September 1915. During this time he was awarded the Military Cross for continuing to observe while being attacked by a German aeroplane at Loos. He was a pilot in No. 3 Squadron in spring 1916 and was taken prisoner on 16 July 1916, after a forced landing behind German lines. He managed to escape from Clausthal Camp, but was recaptured on the Dutch frontier. He later escaped into Switzerland after eighteen nights' walking. In February 1918, he was in command of No. 142 Squadron in Palestine where he was captured by the Turks. Evans returned to Egypt after the Armistice. He was awarded a bar to MC for his numerous attempts to escape. He is best known as the author of *The Escaping Club*.

Lieutenant Anselme Marchal
Marchal was a French pilot in the First World War, remembered for his courageous flight over Berlin in June 1916. He tried to escape from prison three times, successfully escaping on 24 February 1918 with his friend Roland Garros. He was awarded the Légion d'honneur and the Croix de

Guerre for his efforts in the war. He is the author of the book *Après mon vol au-dessus de Berlin*, published in 1919.

Edwin T. Woodhall

Woodhall was born in 1886 and, accomplishing his ambition, joined the London Metropolitan Police in 1906. He progressed through the ranks to the Special Political Branch, then to MI5, the Secret Intelligence Police and finally Protective Surveillance. Due to his exceptional skills in espionage he captured Percy Toplis (the 'Monocled Mutineer') without assistance in the First World War.

Esmee Sartorius

On the outbreak of the war, Sartorius applied to the St John Ambulance. She was sent out to Brussels in Belgium. She was a dedicated and brave nurse, being awarded the 1914 Star. Sartorius returned to England and carried on working as a nurse for the Red Cross until 1918.

Sir Philip Gibbs

Gibbs was born in Kensington, London, to a civil servant. He was home schooled and wished to become a writer. During the First World War, he worked as one of the five official British reporters. However, censorship was soon imposed; Gibbs refused to return and was shortly arrested and brought back home. During the war, he produced many newspaper articles and several books, and in 1920 was awarded a knighthood.

Duncan Grinnell-Milne

Captain Grinnell-Milne, a pilot in the First and Second World Wars, was born in Bromley in London and educated at the University of Freiburg. He was originally enlisted in the 5th Battalion, Rifle Brigade, but was considered too young, at the age of 17, for active service, so was transferred to the 7th Battalion, Royal Fusiliers. He transferred to the RFC in July 1915 and gained his wings. Engine trouble, while over enemy lines, caused him to be taken prisoner in the same year. His story opens in the spring of 1918, just after he had returned to England after two-and-a-half years in a German prison camp. He was awarded the Military Cross and Distinguished Flying Cross and bar for his war efforts.

H.G. Durnford

Durnford's story is about the famous Holzminden Tunnel, by which twenty-nine English officers escaped from a German prison: the Great War's 'Great Escape'. Owing to the tunnel caving in, the remainder of the men were unable to get away. The author took part in this dramatic incident but did not make his escape. He was later removed to Stralsund

Prison in company with two other officers who had also failed in the Holzminden attempt.

Marthe McKenna

Marthe McKenna, then Marthe Cnockaert, was a Belgian girl who witnessed too much of the looting, destruction, and wanton brutality of the German invasion in August 1914. She was generous enough to serve as a hospital nurse, and earned the high regard of the German medical authorities. However, what she had seen and the harsh discipline of the oppressor that she, her parents, and their neighbours were all experiencing, inspired her to undertake the audacious career of a spy. For two years Marthe was 'Laura' of the Anglo-Belgian Intelligence system. She was brave and ingenious, and but for one of those small, fatal slips, which have destroyed so many espionage careers, she might have continued her daring and invaluable 'side-line' until the Armistice. Unfortunately, she was detected, convicted, and condemned to death. Because of her splendid nursing record, and the tireless devotion she had shown hundreds of enemy wounded and sick, her sentence was commuted to imprisonment. And so this heroine, and she was surely that in two capacities, survived until the military prison door swung wide in Belgium. Afterwards, she married a British officer, and took up residence in Westrozebeke, where she composed her memoirs.

Walter Wood

Wood, from Blackburn, Lancashire, served as a private in the 1st/7th Lancashire Fusiliers. As part of the operations in Gallipoli, it was decided to bombard and attack a very strongly fortified Turkish position near Suvla Bay. The frontal attack was a desperate enterprise, as the Turks had dug themselves in, in two lines of trenches of exceptional strength. The attack was made on the afternoon of 21 August 1915, after a bombardment by battleships and heavy land batteries. It was in the course of this advance that the teller of this story, Trooper Frederick William Owen Potts, of the 1/1st Berkshire Yeomanry (Territorial Force), was struck down, and later performed the unparalleled act for which he was awarded the Victoria Cross. For nearly fifty hours Trooper Potts remained under the Turkish trenches with a severely wounded and helpless comrade, 'although he could himself have returned to safety', says the official record. Finally the trooper, in the extraordinary manner which he now describes, saved his comrade's life. Trooper Potts was only 22 years old at the time, and was the first Yeoman to win the most coveted of all distinctions.

CHAPTER ONE

TRAPPED IN BELGIUM

By Harry Beaumont

On the morning of 24 August, 1914, the first day of the Retreat from Mons, I have a very hazy recollection of being put out of action by the combination of a German shell and a brick wall. I was picked up about twenty-four hours later and taken to a hospital by Belgian civilians. I was put to bed there suffering from a slight wound in the groin, and concussion from which I recovered in a week.

The hospital was at the pit head of a colliery in the village of Wasmes, about 7 miles south-west of Mons, and the staff consisted of one nurse, two doctors (both very old) and a few voluntary workers of both sexes. The leader of this little band was named D'Capiaux, a young Belgian engineer, who had been educated in England, and spoke very good English.

There were about forty British patients, most of whom were officers and NCOs, and there was also one German patient, a Prussian. Things were very disorganised just then, and it was some days before the Germans noticed our hospital. They were too busy elsewhere; but they soon took over control, and we British automatically became 'Prisoners of War'. They made the Belgians responsible for supplying us with food and medical comforts, but there was very little of either available. Most of the patients were in a pretty bad way, and six out of eight amputation cases died of tetanus. A German doctor used to come visiting, and after one of these visits a few men were transferred to prison camps in Germany; but I always managed to be absent when he came round, so I stayed on.

The hospital was unguarded, as every man was supposed to be incapable of escape, and the responsibility for our safe custody was placed upon the Belgians.

The hospital authorities gave me the job of nursing one of the British officers. He was totally paralysed, and the Belgians could do very little for him. I nursed him until he died about three weeks later.

Doing this kind of work made me helpful to the Belgians, and they used to give me the tip whenever the German officer came visiting. He always commenced at the officers' building, and by the time he arrived at our end my bed was rolled up and stowed away in the storeroom, and I was well hidden in the scrap-iron yard.

I went on dodging this fellow up to about the second or third week in October; then, one day, he checked the roll and suddenly discovered there was one man in that hospital that he had never seen. He was in a terrible rage and ordered the Belgians to search the colliery and produce me. They knew, of course, where to find me, and I was taken before him. He glared at me, and in very good English said: 'Why have you been absent from this hospital every time I've visited it?' I made the first excuse that came into my head: 'I didn't know you were coming. I'm fond of fresh air and spend most of my time in the grounds.' He said: 'Fresh air! Fresh air! You'll get all the fresh air you want very soon! I shall send you to Stettin-on-Oder!' I said: 'Thank you,' and returned to my ward with something to think about.

I made up my mind then and there that I was not going to Stettin, but I had not the slightest idea what to do about it. Next day the answer came without my seeking. Lance-Corporal Arthur Heath, of my regiment – who was one of the patients – had got very friendly with a Belgian and his wife by the name of Neusy, who used to visit the hospital. Heath took me into his confidence. He told me that if he could get to the Neusys' house they were going to look after him, and get him out of the country when he was well enough.

He was shot through the thigh and could not walk. Someone therefore would have to carry him from the hospital to the Neusys' house, and I was the man he chose to do the job. I said I would do it, but would the Neusys look after me, too? Heath said he did not know, but thought it would be all right. We then started getting ready. Heath practised walking up and down the ward with a couple of sticks, and I looked round for a civilian suit.

Our ward was opposite the gas retorts, and the stoker used to come in about 8 o'clock every night, change into overalls, and hang his suit up near the door. He worked until about 3 o'clock in the morning, and would then fall asleep until it was time to go home; so that suit was mine for the taking. On 26 October we were suddenly ordered to be in readiness to proceed to Germany at 10 o'clock on the following day, so there was now no time to be lost, and we fixed 4 o'clock in the morning as the time for our escape. We arranged that as I was to do all the hard work I should go to bed and Heath would keep awake and rouse me about ten minutes to four.

I have already told you that one of the patients in the hospital was a Prussian, and this Prussian was in our ward. He was badly wounded, and seldom went to sleep, and I was very much afraid that he would see us going and give the alarm. But a funny thing happened. That night he beckoned me to his bedside to help him turn over, which I had often done before. As soon as I had made him comfortable, to my surprise he gripped me by the hand and placed his finger on his lips. This was his way of telling me that he knew what was going on and would keep silent. It was decent of him; we were just brothers in distress.

At ten minutes to four I was roused by Heath, who quietly left the ward on his crutches. I saw him clear and then went to the stokehold and bagged the stoker's suit. I emptied everything out of the pockets and tied them up in a bundle in the old chap's red handkerchief and left it on the hook beside him. I did not want to rob him of more than I could help. He was still dreaming about the end of the war when I crept away.

I joined Heath at the gate. He had discarded his crutches for his sticks, which had been put there for him overnight.

The Neusys' house was about 4 miles away, and we had a rough sketch of the road to it on a sheet of ordinary notepaper. I carried Heath on my back; but it was no fun for him either, as he was in great pain. At every turn of the road we struck a match and consulted our map. I well remember those matches; they were the old-fashioned twinklers of the 'wait a minute' kind. After two hours we reached our destination, which was the second house with iron railings in the Rue Calvary in the village of Petite Wasmes. We hadn't been able to warn the Neusys that we were coming, and we found the outer gate was locked. So I scaled the wall and threw some gravel at the bedroom window. After two or three throws Neusy put out his head, and in a few moments we were inside.

Emil Neusy was a heavily-built man with a fresh complexion and a jolly disposition. His wife Marie was a slim little woman with the heart of a lion. They seemed pleased to have us, and soon made us comfortable; but the difficulty was conversation. They knew no English, and we knew no French, so we had to talk to one another with our hands, which was a very slow job. However, we were not allowed to rest for long. At about 9 o'clock a Belgian from the hospital arrived in a very excited state, and the Neusys at once hid us behind some thick curtains. They then invited him into the room, and after a long and apparently heated conversation he left the house again. Neusy went out soon after and came back with a cab and took Heath away. I followed almost immediately, led by Neusy's son, a boy of thirteen, who took me to some woods and told me to stay there until he came back for me. After dark that night I was collected and taken to a café on the outskirts of the wood, where I found Heath, who had also spent the day in the woods.

We spent several days together in the woods, returning to the café at night for food and shelter. Heath still suffered great pain from his wound and found it very difficult to move about.

By this time German patrols and the Belgian police had got tired of searching the district for us, so we moved by easy stages to the village of Paturage, where we were put up for a time by a Madame Godart, a friend of the Neusys. We returned to the Neusys' house at the end of November.

By this time the food shortage was acute. Everyone was rationed – except us, of course – but we had many friends by now, and never went short.

We were already beginning to pick up a certain amount of French, which eased our position considerably, and Heath had been attended by a doctor and his wound was now on the mend.

One day Neusy showed me a British rifle and several rounds of ammunition which he had souvenired from the battlefields. I did not think it was a wise souvenir, and said so, and advised him to get rid of it. I told him that if the house was searched it would be his death warrant and possibly that of others as well, and although he would not take this seriously at first I never let the subject drop until the rifle was eventually cemented into the wall under the window-sill of the front bedroom. The room was then repapered to remove any traces of tampering with the walls.

Just before Christmas, 1914, the Germans began to realise that there were a good many British soldiers being hidden by the Belgians in occupied territory, so they issued a warning through the Local Authorities that any British soldier who gave himself up before a certain date would be treated as a prisoner of war; but that if he failed to surrender and was caught he would be shot as a spy whether in uniform or not. It also warned the inhabitants that the penalty for harbouring the enemy was death. I never saw this order, but it was discussed by the Neusys, and they decided to take the risk. So we sat tight.

About the middle of February, 1915, Marie received a visit from the mayor of the district. He said that it had come to his knowledge that two English soldiers were hiding in her house, and that as he was responsible for his district being clear they must go. He said he did not care where they went so long as they left the district. The same night I left for Paturage to live with Madame Godart again. Heath preferred to stay where he was.

A fortnight later a neighbour of the Neusys came round to me there and between fits of weeping told me that the Germans had taken Heath. This was very bad news, and as soon as it got dark that night I moved to a place called La Bouverie, about 5 miles distant, to the house of Madame Godart's mother. This old lady was eighty years of age. At dawn the next morning there was a terrific banging at the front door. I naturally thought the Germans had come for me, and was half-way out of the window when I heard the voices of Heath and Emil Neusy.

Heath had not been caught after all, and this is what had happened at the Neusys' house. At 9 o'clock the previous morning, two German detectives had entered by the back gate. They had given the correct secret signal, which was the opening of the gate three times, which automatically gave three peals on the bell in the kitchen. They had then walked straight into the house, covered Marie Neusy with an automatic, and said: 'You've got English in your house.' Marie had denied this at once, although Heath was in bed in the room above. However, the detectives had wasted no time in argument; one remained with Marie and the other started searching the house. Luckily for Heath he began from the cellar. Heath had heard their conversation and knew he was in a hole. He had no time to put on his clothes, so in only his shirt and socks he climbed out of the landing window and dropped on to the roof of the scullery, which jutted out from the kitchen. Unfortunately the slates of the roof gave way with a fearful crash, and Heath nearly came through into the scullery. The German in the kitchen at once rushed to the back door. So did Marie. She got there first, turned the key in the lock and put her back to the door. There was a brief struggle and then the German pushed her aside and opened the door. Unfortunately – or fortunately – this was the moment chosen by Heath to jump off the roof. He jumped on top of the detective and they fell to the ground. Heath was up first and raced down the garden, zig-zagging from side to side, his shirt flapping in the wind. The German who was still on the ground fired four shots at him, but never got a hit. Heath jumped a low wall into the neighbour's garden, at the top of which was another wall – a high one with glass on top. He leapt at this, but missed his hold.

By this time the German was after him and had reached the bottom of Neusy's garden, only a few feet away. He covered Heath with his automatic and said: 'Hands up!' Heath took no notice. He decided not to be an Englishman at any price. The German gave the order again, this time in French and up went Heath's hands.

Meanwhile the German inside the house had reached the landing window and saw what was happening outside. He at once started to shout orders to the one in the garden, who turned round to reply. This gave

Heath another chance. He made one more leap at the wall, gained a hold and was over the top. The German in the garden turned round just in time to see his last leg disappearing. He had one more shot, but was far too late.

Heath had then done a record sprint across a ploughed field, down a lane, and through a forge, until he came to a cottage. The back door stood invitingly open, so in he went and locked the door behind him. The good lady of the house came down from upstairs and had a bit of a shock to find a stranger with no trousers on seated in her kitchen. However, he explained his position, and she soon fixed him up with one of her husband's suits. Heath had left the house at dark and gone to Madame Godart's, where he found Neusy. They had remained there until next morning, when they came to me.

Marie Neusy was arrested and taken to Mons, where she was committed for trial. The Germans ripped her house to pieces and took away several hundred francs. They didn't, however, find that rifle, and for all I know it's there still. They left word with the maid that if Emil Neusy came to Mons for his money he could have it. He went next day and they arrested him, too.

After a few days at La Bouverie we returned to Madame Godart, where we anxiously awaited the result of the trial. Marie smuggled a letter to us from her prison concealed in a piece of bread, in which she said we were not to worry about her, for what she had done was for her country and not for us. These were brave words from a woman who was expecting her death.

But when the trial eventually came off, the first witness, who was Marie's maid, a girl of only twelve, stated with great presence of mind that the man who had escaped was a Belgian, and that he was the lover of Madame Neusy, and stayed in the house when the master was away on business. As soon as Neusy heard this he jumped up in court and demanded a divorce and acted the part of the wronged husband so well that as the Germans had no evidence to the contrary they had to accept the story. Marie was sentenced to one month's imprisonment for obstructing the police, and Neusy was charged the costs of the trial.

A few days later we were visited by D'Capiaux, the engineer from the hospital, and I learnt what happened there when we escaped. He said the Germans were furious, and fined everyone connected with the hospital, and removed all the prisoners into Germany. He then told us that he had made arrangements to get us away. He took our photographs, and presented us next day with a certificate of identity, which changed our nationality to Belgian. This certificate was an absolute forgery, but complete in every detail, even to the police stamp. He had even gone so far as to append our signatures without ever having seen our handwriting.

In a few days a guide came for us and we left for Brussels, where we were taken to a hospital. The matron in charge of this hospital was Nurse Edith Cavell. I'm afraid I can't tell you much about Nurse Cavell. She was very busy all the time, and so we didn't see very much of her, but she seemed a very homely woman with a smile and a cheery word for everyone.

Brussels was teeming with Germans, and here under their noses were at least a score of helpless British Tommies waiting to be smuggled across the frontier.

We were in the hospital for only three days, and then there was a sudden alarm, and we were all cleared out in twos and threes, and conducted to the homes of various Belgians, who were all members of the same wonderful organisation. This organisation was linked up from Northern France, right across Belgium to the Dutch frontier, and existed solely for the purpose of helping British, French and Belgians out of the country.

In this sudden move I was separated from Heath, and left the hospital accompanied by Michael Carey, of the Munster Fusiliers. The Munsters were cut off during the Retreat from Mons, and many of them had remained at large until picked up by the organisation.

A week later we left our house in the Avenue de Longchamps with a guide and made an attempt to reach the frontier. On the way we picked up four more Irishmen, which made our party seven, and we soon left Brussels behind and reached the open country. The order of march was for the guide to go ahead and the remainder to follow in pairs at intervals of 200 yards.

We passed through Louvain and Aerschot, and in the late afternoon arrived at the Monastery of Averabode, where we received food and shelter for the night. There were over 200 monks in this monastery and only two could speak English.

The next morning our party was joined by a young Belgian who also wanted to get out of the country. We set off at daybreak, left the main road, and made our way across country. Our destination was Turnout, a town near the Dutch frontier. At about mid-day we came to a railway crossing, where a sentry examined our forged identity cards. He just compared the face with the photograph, and allowed us to pass.

The two Belgians, the three Irishmen, and myself got through without a hitch; but one of the Irishmen of the last pair could not for the moment find his identity card, and while he was fumbling in his pockets, he accidentally dropped a 5-franc note. No sooner had it reached the ground than the sentry promptly put his foot on it, looked round at the guard-house behind to see that no one was watching, and passed the Irishman on with a movement of the hand. That was accidental bribery.

Two hours later we struck the main road again, and here our guide gave instructions to the other Belgian and left us. Soon afterwards we entered Turnout, which was packed with Germans.

We at once proceeded to the address which had been given us of the man who was the next link in the chain of the organisation. But when we got there we found, to our dismay, that the house was full of German soldiers. It had been taken over as a billet. This floored us; our guide had gone and we had no other addresses, so we retired to a café in a quiet part of the town to discuss the situation.

The Belgian made enquiries as to the possibility of our crossing the frontier by ourselves, but he was told that we should have to swim a canal and pass two chains of sentries, which was considered an impossibility without an experienced guide.

It was very dangerous to remain in Turnout, so the only thing to do was to return to Brussels. We were all footsore and weary after our two days' march, but we found an old woman with a horse and cart, and she agreed to take the risk and give us a lift back to the monastery of Averabode for the sum of 12 francs 50 cents per head.

As soon as it was dark we set off, and got along all right until we were halted by a mounted patrol at about 1 o'clock. I was on the front seat, and the officer in charge of the patrol walked up to me with an electric torch and a revolver, both of which he pointed at me. He questioned me in Flemish, which I didn't understand, so I kept my mouth shut. The old woman and the Belgian butted in, with explanations, and we were ordered off the cart and lined up by the roadside, where our identity cards were examined. The officer seemed satisfied with these, and allowed us to pass on our way.

It was a narrow shave, for there were three things we should have been caught out on. Only two of the party had spoken at all; we were on the road during prohibited hours without a special permit; and we were many miles from the place of our registration.

We arrived at the monastery four hours later, and when we had had some food turned in for a well needed rest. That evening the Belgian left us to return to Brussels, and promised to report our position to Nurse Cavell.

We were well treated by the monks. We slept in the laundry at night, and retired to a room at the top of the building by day, where we passed away the time by playing cards for buttons. We couldn't play for money as the cost of our journey back from Turnout had 'broke' the lot of us.

Seven days passed and no word came from Brussels, so one of the monks volunteered to go in and find out what was to be done. He returned the next day with the guide who had conducted us to Turnout.

The following day we returned to Brussels. Michael Carey and myself were taken to another house in the Rue du Brasserie. The other four Irishmen went somewhere else, and I never saw them again.

Our hostess was a very wealthy woman. Her house was stocked with everything of the best, and for eight days we lived like lords. Then, with two Frenchmen who were already in the house when we arrived, we were picked up by the same old guide and made another attempt to reach the frontier. We passed up through Malines this time, and everything went smoothly until we reached an examining post at a bridge-head over a canal, about 6 miles south of Antwerp. There were two sentries, one on each side of the road. The guide had already passed, and the Frenchmen were following behind Carey and myself. We looked at the two sentries as we approached, and weighed them up carefully. The fellow on the right looked less intelligent that the other, so we decided to give him the honour of inspecting our identity cards. He just compared the face with the photograph and allowed us to pass.

A little farther on, round a bend in the road, we waited for the two Frenchmen to catch up. We waited ten minutes and then our guide became alarmed and went back to see what had happened. He learnt that the two Frenchmen had been arrested by the sentry on the left. They had identity cards the same as ourselves and we never knew the reason for their arrest or their fate. It was just luck that had made us choose the sentry on the right instead of the one on the left.

When we reached Antwerp we found our next link, which was a Red Cross building which had been used during the siege. The building was empty, however, and the man in charge told us that it was being taken over by the Germans next day as a clearing station for the Belgian refugees who were returning from Holland. This was another disappointment. He allowed us to stay there that night and early next morning our guide took us to the Hotel d'Esperance, which soon belied its name. This was on a Saturday towards the end of April, six months after I'd escaped from the hospital at Wasmes.

After we had some lunch our guide told us to remain where we were until he returned on Monday. He said we had nothing to worry about; that everything had been arranged and there was nothing to pay. On Sunday night the proprietress presented us with the bill, which included the cost of the guide's food for the day before. As this took place in the public dining-room, and there were a good many Germans there, we couldn't argue the point, so we retired to our bedroom followed by the proprietress, and induced her to wait for her money until our friend returned on Monday. I needn't add we never saw him again. There were further arguments with the proprietress on the Monday and Tuesday, and the good lady informed us that if we didn't pay by 12 o'clock on Wednesday she'd inform the police. I'm pretty certain she'd have done this at once if she'd known who we were. Carey and I couldn't muster 5 francs between us, and our position was serious. On the Wednesday morning I told her I was going out to find my friend. Where I really went to was a house nearby, which was tenanted by the American Commission for the relief of the Belgians, but there were too many Germans about the building for my liking, and I returned to the hotel. About 11.30 Carey decided to go round and try his luck. I told him not to return if he was unsuccessful, and that I'd try and make a 'getaway' on my own, but he wouldn't agree to that. He returned just before twelve with a face wreathed in smiles, and I knew he'd been successful. He'd gained audience with the Commissioner, who had given him enough cash to meet our immediate expenses, which we paid without delay, and had promised to help us, too, in other ways. Half an hour later we were visited by a Belgian who owned a café in another part of the city. He said the Commissioner had sent him to look after us until such time as we could be passed over the frontier. The Commission would allow us 20 francs a day, he said, but we were not to visit it again, and any communication was to be made through him.

After this, our prestige at the hotel went up by leaps and bounds; our meals were served in a private room, and there was no more trouble with the proprietress,

We roamed all over Antwerp for three weeks, and then, on 16 May 1915, we were introduced to the guide who was to take us over the frontier. He was a small withered old man over sixty years of age and almost a dwarf. The following night we met at the café of our friend who had been our link with the American Commission, and after cracking the best bottle of champagne in the house, Carey and I and the guide accompanied by the café proprietor boarded a tram for the outskirts of the city. Here our friend bid us Godspeed and returned to his home. It was now 9 o'clock, pitch dark, and raining in torrents. We left the main road and soon realised that our guide was a marvel. In spite of his age he moved quickly, in fact we had difficulty in keeping pace with him. He could see like a cat, and appeared to know every inch of the country. After three hours of zig-zagging down railway tracks, wading ditches, and trespassing over private property, we emerged from some undergrowth by a deserted cottage, and saw the frontier barrier a few feet ahead. It was still raining heavily and we were soaked to the skin. The church clocks in Holland were striking midnight, and we could see the electric lights on the Dutch roads 500 yards away. Our guide motioned us to lie down, and left us for about ten minutes. When he returned he took off all his clothes except his shirt, under-pants and boots, and told us to do the same. This was to make it easier for us to crawl through the wire. We tied up our discarded clothes and threw them over the top of the barrier, which appeared to be 15 to 20 feet in width. It was thickly meshed and very close to the ground. Each of us then selected a spot and commenced to crawl through. This could only be done by lying flat on the stomach, stretching the arms at full length, grasping the wire and pulling the body forward two or three inches at a time. It took us quite twenty minutes to reach the other side. My underclothes were ripped to ribbons and my body smarted from head to foot where it had been torn by the barbs. We rested a few moments, then grabbed our bundles and made a bolt towards the lights in the distance. About 500 yards further on we waded a ditch, stepped over a couple of strands of barbed wire, and saw a sentry in blue uniform a few yards away. We were in Holland. The sentry came up, patted us on the back and said: 'Goot Engleesh'. We put on our clothes and an hour later were being cared for at a Dutch inn.

The following morning our wonderful guide, who had taken us through without having seen or heard a German sentry, handed us over to the Belgian Consul at Roosendael and bade us goodbye. These guides were paid by the organisation at the rate of three pounds a head for every one they got safely across. The same day we were sent to Flushing, and when I was signing my name in the Strand Hotel register I saw the signature of Arthur Heath, whom I'd left in Brussels. A day later I caught him up at Rotterdam, and we both came home together on 21 May 1915. This was the end of my journey.

I had been told by the guide who took me from Nurse Cavell's hospital that I was known as No. 83 on her books; but out of that number I was only the thirteenth to get safely across the frontier.

You may like to know what eventually happened to some of the principals of this story.

D'Capiaux, who forged the identity cards, was sentenced to twenty years' imprisonment just after Nurse Cavell was shot. He was released at the Armistice.

Emil and Marie Neusy left the country and came to England as refugees in August, 1915. They were afterwards compensated by the British Government. Marie Neusy and Madame Godart received special medals and illuminated addresses from both the British and Belgian Governments.

As for me, I was officially reported by the War Office as killed in action on 24 August 1914, and when I reached England I found my wife a widow.

CHAPTER TWO

MY FIRST ESCAPE FROM RUHLEBEN

By WALLACE ELLISON

First thought seriously of escaping from Germany when I found myself in the Stadt Vogtei Prison, Berlin, in the spring of 1915. I had played with the idea before, but the difficulties in the way seemed at first almost insuperable. I was interned, along with other Englishmen living in Germany, in Ruhleben Camp, which is situated between Berlin and Spandau, more than 300 miles, as the crow flies, from the Dutch frontier.

Once ideas had begun to take definite shape in my mind, I lived only for the moment when I could put them into execution. I thrilled at the prospect as a boy thrills at the thought of his first love. Sweet, indeed, are the uses of adversity.

Now all this rendered necessary a fairly thorough knowledge of conditions in Germany beyond the last barbed wire fence of the camp, and this knowledge could only be arrived at by dint of much patient and cautious inquiry. A chauffeur in camp lent me a Michelin guide-book, which proved to be a great boon, and although little detail was given, one was able to get a fairly good idea of the general nature of the country through which one might have to pass. Much was also learned from conversations in camp, though a good deal of the information obtained in this way proved to be of very little practical value. The most valuable information was obtained by casually chatting with those of our German guards who had recently returned from leave, and it was a great opportunity to get into touch with a soldier who, while on leave, had travelled in the direction of the Dutch frontier. Such a man, when questioned in an innocent manner, was often able to clear up such doubtful points as strictness or laxity of control by detectives on long-distance trains travelling in the direction of the frontier.

Had I taken advantage of the few little privileges granted me as barrack captain I should doubtless have found it easier to escape from Ruhleben

Camp than I could as an ordinary interned prisoner. Feeling, however, that it would not be playing the game to make a wrong use of these privileges, I decided to abandon my intention to escape as long as I remained in that position.

In April, 1915, when I ventured to oppose the German camp officers on what I regarded – and still regard – as an important matter of principle, I was informed by Baron von Taube, the Commandant of the camp, that I was being taken to prison for the purpose of trial. Two corporals, armed with rifles, escorted me to Berlin, and handed me over to the warders of the Stadt Vogtei Prison. The prison authorities were informed later that I had been sent 'for punishment' – not for trial – and that I had to be kept in the strictest form of solitary confinement for an indefinite period. All my letters of inquiry and of protest remained unanswered.

While in the prison yard one day for exercise, I met a Scotsman, Henry Kirkpatrick, originally from Dumfries, and chief engineer of the Union Cold Storage Co., Ltd. He had just arrived in prison after having made a very plucky escape from Ruhleben a fortnight before. Although fifty-two years of age, he had been the first among 4,000 men to attempt to escape from Ruhleben and after a very adventurous fourteen days' tramp had somehow or other become separated from his companion, who spoke perfect colloquial German. At this stage of his adventures he was only about 30 miles from the Dutch frontier, and the previous night had fainted from exhaustion in front of an inn in a small village. He recovered and pressed on, however, before any one saw him, but in passing through the outskirts of Cloppenburg the following morning he was overtaken by a gendarme on a bicycle and at once arrested.

A lasting friendship grew up between us. Our cells were on the same level on two sides of a corner, and we would frequently whistle to each other, climb up behind the bars of our windows, and hold long surreptitious conversations condoling with each other about our poor empty stomachs, and through the iron bars discuss the details of his escape. I learned much from him of conditions in Berlin and Germany from an escaper's point of view.

At the end of my five weeks' detention I bade farewell to Kirkpatrick. The American Embassy had succeeded in procuring my release from prison, and I was sent back to camp. It was still winter when I was sent to prison, but when the day of my release came it was already spring. A Berlin policeman escorted me from the prison by train through Charlottenburg to Spandau and Ruhleben, and I remember vividly his amazement as he contemplated my childish delight at the sight of fresh green grass and the luscious green of budding trees. I cannot remember sheer force of contrast ever having touched my senses with such feelings of delight, unless it be that supreme moment when, on the night of 13 November 1917, I waded through the last frontier canal, and climbed, a free man, on to neutral soil at the other side.

Two of my friends in camp were Mr E. Falk and Mr Geoffrey Pyke, whose plucky escape from Ruhleben Camp has been recorded in *Black-wood's Magazine* and in Mr Pyke's book *To Ruhleben and Back*. For a time we were practically pledged to each other to escape together. We met at all hours of the day, and in all sorts of places in camp, for the purpose of discussing plans and consulting maps and newspapers.

For a long time the question of greatest importance was that of choosing the most suitable route. We ruled the Swiss frontier, both in Austria and Germany, out of the question, partly on account of the great distance which would have to be covered in order to get there, and partly because we had very little information concerning either of these two frontiers. The two others which remained were the routes to Denmark and to Holland. The route to Denmark by land, had we chosen it, would have meant covering almost as much distance as that from Berlin to the Dutch frontier, and, further, presented two definite objections. The first was the difficulty of crossing the Kiel Canal, and the second was the presence in Schleswig-Holstein, at that time, of a very considerable number of German troops. The frontier was, moreover, only a short one, and comparatively easy to guard. The prospect, on the other hand, of escaping by boat across the Baltic to Denmark appealed very strongly to us, and it was long before we decided to abandon this idea and centre all our thoughts on plans for reaching the Dutch frontier.

Our idea, had we chosen the northern route, was to have tramped the whole distance to the Baltic coast, lying up during the day and walking only by night. On arrival there we should have endeavoured to evade the vigilance of the coastguards, steal a fishing-boat, and row or sail across the narrow straits which separate Denmark from Germany to the north of the small peninsula known as the Zingst. The danger of arriving on the coast, however, and finding it impossible when there to procure a boat of any kind, led us to rule the Danish route out of our reckoning.

When the date of our departure was drawing near I had a strong pre-sentiment – I can give it no more definite name – that three were one too many for such an enterprise, and I decided to drop out. My two friends escaped, spent about a fortnight *en route*, and succeeded in crossing the Dutch frontier on 24th July 1915. When I look back on their success and on my failure at the time, I do not regret my decision, for, after all, it was infinitely better that two out of three should escape rather than that three should be captured.

As soon as they had gone I set to work on fresh plans along with another man who lived in the same horse-box – a British subject by naturalisation, who spoke perfect German and had a thorough knowledge of the country and the ways of the German people. I had not at that time a thorough knowledge of German, and my accent was quite pronouncedly an English one. From this point of view, my companion, with his perfect German, made an admirable second. His skill in conducting the most delicate negotiations drew from me unstinted admiration. Often he went to parlous lengths. He had a very winning way with the German guards, and, not lacking funds, soon procured one or two willing helpers among them. I expressed strong disapproval from time to time, but he had always such excellent reasons and was so confident of success that I ended by holding my tongue and giving him a free hand. We were taking time by the forelock and making sure of the German indemnity – in services rendered.

After our recapture – for we were recaptured – we strongly and most indignantly denied that we had bribed any one. Now that the military power of Germany has been broken, I can admit that we had – in fact, we bribed several German soldiers, and, so slippery is the path of wrong-doing, I think we should have bribed the Commandant himself if we had thought he would have accepted our bribe, and, most important of all, if we had thought that we would get value for our money.

Our plan of escape gradually grew into a triumph of perfect organisation. My friend, in his implicit belief in the almighty mark, bribed to get money brought into the camp; bribed to get things which we should need on our journey smuggled out of camp to addresses in Berlin where we could pick them up; bribed to have things brought into camp – in fact, bribery became the order of the day. My qualms of conscience eventually disappeared entirely, and I came to look upon it all as a matter of course. By further largesse he almost succeeded in making our escape a kind of personally conducted Cook's or Polytechnic tour; and I think he would be the first to admit, now that the war is a thing of the past, that his unlimited belief in the efficacy of money leg, at the last moment, to our undoing.

To my amazement, he succeeded in working up friendly relations with an enemy soldier in the camp, whose brother, the soldier said, was a horse-dealer. I met the brother later, and should say he was probably a horse-stealer. In any event, he was reputed to have a fairly intimate knowledge of frontier conditions, and the soldier claimed that his brother had several times brought horses and cattle from Holland over the Dutch frontier into Germany. One part of the Dutch frontier he claimed to know particularly well, and E— bribed the soldier to arrange terms with the brother for a personally conducted tour from Berlin to Holland. The brother was agreeable, on terms, and it was not long before E— had the whole scheme complete. Our scoundrel of a guard also undertook, for a further consideration, to be instrumental in allowing us to escape from the camp.

I lived, along with my companion and three others, in a horse-box in Stable No. 4, and it was usual for the corporal and soldier in charge of our barrack to come round at bed-time and count the inmates of each box. About a fortnight prior to our escape, E— threw a mosquito-net over his bed each night when he went to sleep, and I fixed a curtain on a wire in front of my bunk. The two of us made a pretence of slipping into bed, dressed or undressed, when we heard the corporal begin his round; I drew my curtain, E— let down his mosquito-net, and when the corporal and soldier arrived to count us, one of our box-mates whispered: 'They are both in bed.'

This we kept up for a fortnight, and as the idea of either of us attempting to escape had not entered the corporal's mind, he went away, night after night, quite satisfied. We concluded that we should in this way make sure of a long start before our escape from camp was discovered.

There was much to recommend the policy of attempting to reach the Dutch frontier by means of a short railway journey and a long tramp; but eventually we decided to make a quick dash for Holland, and had we not been captured on the Dutch frontier, we should have succeeded in reaching Holland and freedom within less than thirty-six hours. As a matter of fact, the day Falk and Pyke, who had been a fortnight on the way, succeeded in crossing the frontier, we, after a journey of less than twenty-four hours, were captured there. This would surely have been a record escape, in point of view of time.

In those days it was usual for volunteer working gangs to go out of Ruhleben dragging carts, accompanied by a German soldier, for the purpose of bringing into the camp manure, gravel, and soil for the camp gardens. As it was desirable for us to escape from camp in the early afternoon, so as to be able to leave Berlin that night, we were glad to avail ourselves of the opportunity of escaping with the help of one of these gangs. Good men and true were plentiful in a camp like Ruhleben, and it was the work of only a few hours to get together a working gang of men who could be trusted to see little and say less. A pretext was found for taking a cart out of the camp to get gravel for the camp gardens, and if there were any observant people close to the main gates about 4 o'clock on the afternoon of 23 July 1915, they were probably astonished to see E— and myself strenuously helping, for the first time, to drag a cart through the open gates into the road which ran past the front of the camp.

Fortunately for us, the sentry at the main gate and the sentry accompanying the cart neglected to count the men who passed through. Our first trip with the cart was to an open field which lay between the railway and the road running from Berlin to Spandau. Escape there proved to be entirely out of the question. The sentry was, of course, our own pet scoundrel, and in himself was no obstacle to our escape, but the presence of so many Englishmen close to the main road attracted the attention of a considerable number of passers-by, including several German officers, who watched us very closely. Our movements, too, may have aroused some suspicion, for I saw a railway official dodge from bush to bush on the railway embankment and watch us very closely.

We started a complaint that the sort of soil we were getting was quite unsuitable for our purpose, and persuaded the sentry to allow us to load up with fresh soil in a field much more quietly situated on the other side of the camp. The whole time E— and I kept as much in the background as possible, in order that the sentry might afterwards have an excuse for not having noticed our absence on the return of the rest of the party to camp. I confess that I felt the whole time most ill at ease. I knew the sentry was not to be trusted, and quite expected that he would betray us when we attempted to move away from the gang.

The road to the field we had in mind led along the fringe of a wood at the eastern end of the camp, and then, taking a sharp turn to the left, passed over a small wooden bridge. When we reached the bridge my companion and I moved to the tail-end of the party, and as the men turned to the left to go over the bridge into the field we slowed down, and as soon as the cart was out of sight walked away at an easy pace in the opposite direction.

Our road led us past the electricity works and then on to the main road leading to Berlin. In accordance with our carefully considered plans, E— was to do all the talking, and I had to speak only when absolutely compelled by questioning to do so. In fact, we had gone to the length of smuggling into the camp an ear trumpet, by means of which I was to persuade people, while we were passing through Germany, that I was almost stone deaf. After a little consideration, however, we decided not to use it, as we felt that it might attract too much attention. We thought it better that I should dress and look as far as possible like a German student on holiday, and, to this end, the day before our escape I got the camp barber to shear off all my hair. In England I should have looked like a criminal; in Germany the ruse helped me to look like a German university student. To complete my costume I had bought a pair of round horn-rimmed spectacles and a so-called Schiller shirt.

When we had left the cart and the bridge about 100 yards behind us I removed my glasses, put on the horn spectacles, turned the white collar of the German Schiller shirt which I was wearing so as to have it outside my jacket collar, altered the shape of my hat so as to make it look as German as possible, and turned down the bottoms of my trousers, which when turned up looked far too English in cut. If I did not look like a young German university student on holiday, I must certainly have looked like a cheerful lunatic who had just escaped from an asylum. However, we were enjoying the first snatch of freedom we had known for many months. The experience had all the glory and freshness of a dream. Free!

We were walking along the main road leading to Berlin, still fairly close to the camp, when my friend whispered, 'Lookout!' and I saw, to my dismay, that the carriage which conveyed the German officers to and from the camp was approaching along the highroad. It passed us within a yard, but was fortunately empty, save for the driver, who eyed us very closely, but nevertheless drove on. We jumped on to a tram at the Spandauer Bock, and while we were sitting at the back of the tram passed a German corporal from the camp, who, to our amusement, saluted my companion, doubtless in the belief that E— was going to Berlin on special leave. A pretty girl had to stand while we were sitting, and I had sternly to repress a desire to offer her my seat. 'Remember, you are now a German,' I kept repeating to myself. On the way to the city we left the tram, caught a taxi, and drove to the centre of Berlin.

My friend, as behoves the leader of a personally conducted tour, had, of course, arranged for apartments in Berlin, and we instructed the taxi-driver to take us to the corner of a street fairly close to the house we wanted. We were quite well received there, and early that evening the soldier's brother arrived. His first desire was to get hold of the money we had promised him, and only then would he discuss further plans. We handed over the money, but found, to our chagrin, that he had only the most confused notions of the best method of procedure. In any event, it was clear that we had to leave Berlin that night and travel to Duisburg, Crefeld, and Geldern, a small village quite close to the Dutch frontier. He assured us that he knew the rest of the way, and hinted at arrangements which he had made on the spot with a sergeant among the frontier guards stationed at the village of Walbeck on the actual frontier line.

It all sounded very vague and unsatisfactory. He looked a scoundrel, and at a time when the overwhelming majority of Germans were fiercely patriotic he was willing to stoop to so dirty a business. This in itself did not concern or worry us, as we were bent on reaching Holland by hook or by crook. All this meant, however, that we could place very little confidence in him, and our realisation of this fact added to our vague sense of uneasiness. Before he left we decided on the train by which we should travel from the Friedrichstrasse station, he, of course, agreeing to travel in another part of the train as though he had no connection whatsoever with us.

II

We left that night by an express train from one of the main stations in Berlin – the Friedrichstrasse Bahnhof – and had managed to secure two tickets for sleeping berths. Our idea in doing so was not to travel in as great luxury as possible, but to avoid any possible control by detectives on the way; and we thought it much more likely that we should be able to do so, and at the same time avoid embarrassing questions from fellow-passengers, if we travelled by sleeper rather than second or third class. We were right in our conjecture. My friend, to whom I left all the talking on account of his perfect command of the language, left me in our compartment, and shortly afterwards came back and assured me that he had arranged everything satisfactorily with the guard. We travelled from Berlin, along the line which runs within about 50 yards of Ruhleben Camp, and laughed quietly to ourselves as we pictured the astonishment and chagrin of the authorities on their discovery of our escape the following day. The journey to Duisburg was uneventful. There we changed, travelled third-class to Crefeld, spent a little time in the town, and then bought tickets for Geldern, a small village which lies within an hour's walk of the Dutch frontier.

We had to run in order to catch our train at Crefeld, and arrived on the platform just as it was moving out. It was thus impossible for us to select a suitable compartment, and we were bundled into a third-class compartment, which, much to our dismay, contained a Prussian railway official and, among other passengers, a German soldier returning on leave from the Eastern front.

In Duisburg we had each bought a copy of the *Kölnische Zeitung*. My companion was very much afraid that my unsatisfactory German would betray me if I were drawn into conversation. He immediately opened his newspaper, glanced at the headlines, read on for a few minutes, and then, leaning over to me, shouted in my ear in German:

'*Die Italiener kriegen wieder ihre Prügel!*' ('The Italians are getting it hot again!')

I nodded vacantly and went on reading my paper. He then fell to discussing the war and Germany's prospects with the Germans in the compartment.

From 1 May 1917, to the end of the war a broad belt of territory on the German side of the Dutch frontier was declared *Sperrgebiet* (forbidden territory), and special passports were issued to persons authorised to travel there. German soldiers were on sentry duty night and day at all railway stations in this area, their duty being to examine the papers of all who passed through. In July, 1915, however, there was no military guard on the station at Geldern, and all that we had to fear was the vigilance of the railway officials and the prying eyes of German civilians.

It was about 10 o'clock in the morning when we arrived at Geldern, and after we had passed out of the station our accomplice, the horse-dealer, joined us, and we set out to walk along the high-road in the direction of the village of Walbeck, which lies on the frontier itself. We passed quite a lot of German soldiers, some on bicycles, some driving, and some on foot, greeted them cheerily when they eyed us with suspicion, and passed on. In the sheer audacity of our plan lay our salvation. It evidently occurred to no one whom we met that any escaped prisoner would be so mad as to walk along a highroad leading to a frontier village, unabashed, in broad daylight.

On arrival at the first inn we skirted the village of Walbeck and, after walking about a quarter of an hour through the fields in a direction running parallel to the Dutch-German frontier, we found fairly good cover in a wood, alongside of which ran a deep country lane or cutting. As soon as we had settled upon our place of concealment until nightfall, our accomplice left us to go back to the village inn, as he said, to confirm arrangements for our safe crossing of the frontier with this German sergeant whom he professed to know. He promised to return within an hour.

There we lay among the tall fronds of bracken and dreamed of our home-coming. The silence of the countryside was unbroken save for the singing of birds, the occasional bark of a dog in some farmyard near, and the shrill voices of children at play. I was very happy, and felt absolutely certain of success. Hour after hour passed, but our accomplice did not return. When he did not put in an appearance I was very relieved, for I would not trust him. According to my calculations, we were about half an hour's walk from Holland and freedom, and I was looking eagerly forward to the final stretch, when we should break cover and start out together on the interesting work of dodging the armed guards who patrolled the frontier. We learned from one of the soldiers who captured us later in the day that from our hiding-place we could almost have thrown a stone over into Holland.

We were not satisfied with our cover, as it was not sufficiently dense to conceal us from any one passing by. About 1 o'clock, therefore, we went deeper into the wood prospecting for better cover, and eventually found what we sought in a clump of bushes close to one edge of the wood, on the side farthest from where we had hidden in the morning. There we lay, listening and waiting. Sometimes we slept peacefully, only to be wakened by the rain which fell from time to time on to our upturned faces.

The failure of our accomplice to put in an appearance worried E— much more than it affected me. After we had been in hiding for some time his genius for negotiation began to assert itself, and he expressed a confidence which amazed me in his ability to return to the village and literally arrange with someone to buy our way across into Holland. He became more and more restless, and did not agree with me that to take the last stretch as a pure adventure offered the best chance of success. It was simply a difference of opinion on a question of policy. He felt convinced that he was right, and I felt convinced, and still do, that I was right. At any other stage of the adventure the consequences of a conflict of opinion might not have been so serious, but at this critical stage perfect unanimity between us was essential. Each man had equal interests at stake, and each realised that neither had a right to dictate any course of action to the other. His desire was that we should both return to the village we had skirted that morning, and see what we could accomplish by negotiation. I protested, on the ground that the game already lay in our hands – that we had only to wait until nightfall, and then cautiously crawl across the belt of open country which lay between us and our goal, that we should be courting disaster if we entered a frontier village crowded with soldiers, and that we had tempted Providence sufficiently with our audacity up to that point. Our views were irreconcilable. He generously suggested that we should each go our own way. The offer was tempting in the extreme, but I recognised that it was largely due to his guidance and his knowledge of the country and the language that we had been able to get so far in so short a time, and I felt I should not be playing the game if I deserted him at that point. He left alone for the village about 4 o'clock in the afternoon, and, at his request, I returned to our former hiding-place in the wood, in order that he might more easily be able to find me on his return.

While he was away the rain came down steadily, and I spent most of my time cutting long fronds of bracken with which I endeavoured to construct a better hiding-place in a dry ditch. My feeling of absolute certainty that all would go well had given place to a sense of vague apprehension, and when E— returned, looking breathless and very agitated, about three-quarters of an hour later, I felt convinced that the game was up.

He told me that he had seen the horse-dealer in the inn, but the latter had not returned to us because he was quite clearly being watched with suspicion, that he had been roughly questioned by a gendarme regarding his presence so near the frontier, and that his papers had been examined. We also learned later that we had been seen by some peasant women while we were walking through the wood back to our first hiding-place, and the information they gave to the military authorities in the village led to our capture.

A last remnant of hope lingered in my heart that all would still go well with us, but before many minutes had passed the rude awakening came. A hefty German soldier dashed, apparently unarmed, through the hedge which separated us from the deep cutting, and came towards us. When about a dozen paces from us caution got the upper hand, and he turned, dashed back through the hedge, and leaped on to the high bank on the other side of the road. There he joined a young fellow, whom we had not noticed before, and, unleashing a police-dog, urged it to attack us. I got behind a tree with the intention of climbing it, when I noticed that the dog, instead of attacking us, was running round in search of rabbits, and there was apparently nothing to fear from that source. The soldier then called out to us: 'Who are you? Have you identification papers?'

We shouted 'Yes!' in order to gain time, and told him we would produce them as soon as he had put the dog again on leash. Eventually he did so, and we joined him in the lane, where my friend produced several German letters, but nothing that was able to satisfy the soldier. He told us that we should have to go to the Army Headquarters in the village of Walbeck. We had not gone many yards before we discovered that we were surrounded by German soldiers armed with rifles, some of whom had rushed up on foot, others on bicycles. It was clear that the game was up, and we informed them that we were civilian Englishmen who had escaped the day before from Ruhleben Camp. We were then marched into the village.

CHAPTER THREE

WINGS OF WRATH

By DUNCAN GRINNELL-MILNE

His Majesty lit a cigarette, inhaled, blew out the match. 'And what are you going to do now?' he asked. He had moved a little to one side whilst lighting that cigarette, so that my eyes were no longer upon his face. I looked out of an open window upon Green Park. The trees were in leaf, a young dog raced over the grass, the sun shone. A faint breeze ruffled the loose-hanging curtains and bore in from Piccadilly and Hyde Park Corner the subdued roar of London, a roar that to my unaccustomed ears was like a distant roll of drums, an eternal call to arms.

'What are you going to do now?'

The King had come forward again, between me and the light, and now his head was framed by the tall window and the green grass beyond. London was behind him. The call to arms came from over his shoulder.

'I'm going back to France, sir.'

I had no hesitation; France it must be. I had given the matter a great deal of thought, and my answer to that particular question was decided upon long before I reached Buckingham Palace. But I have no doubt that, had I been in any uncertainty, those twenty minutes of the King's audience would have compelled me to make up my mind without possibility of change. For the telling of my story had reawakened old voices heard upon the banks of the Lys, in the keen air above Artois, and in the less whole-some air of St. Quentin gaol. And, as I see it, the reasons for such a re-awakening are easy to understand, since after long months of endeavour, of frequent failure and occasional despair, the great, the longed-for, the romantic climax had come. The King had listened to my tale of adventure as he had listened to others before me. Fortune had smiled – if rather late in the day – and the adventure seemed to be concluded.

Seemed – for I saw clearly that it was not yet ended. Real success could only be claimed when I had completed the circle, returned to the point from which I had started …

'I'm going back to France!'

I had caught myself wondering, even before the interview, how the King would receive this declaration of mine. Would he, like certain kindly people at the Air Ministry and elsewhere, say: 'No, no, my boy, you've done enough'? I hoped not. The remark made me shudder, for they were dead who had 'done enough'. Or would he smile appreciation and encourage me to return?

The question that came by way of reply was more to the point. It showed a strangely deep understanding, not only of the attitude of those in authority, but also, I think, of my personal desires and their probable frustration. Just four words:

'Will they let you?'

I would have liked to reply, 'Ay, there's the rub,' but instead I answered meekly that I thought 'they' would. It was not quite true. I did *not* think so. I was beginning to be afraid that 'they' would not let me go. The fear had become more real during the past week or two, but I think it had been growing ever since the afternoon when the train carried me from St Quentin to the Rhine.

*   *   *

That was an afternoon of unalleviated melancholy, of sadness growing more intense at each rhythmical click of the wheels upon the rails. For as long as we were in France some faint hope still beat within me that something would happen – that the train might be derailed, that a bomb might fall from the empty sky to kill my captors, even that a sudden and wholly unexpected offensive by the Allies might sweep through the trench lines into the back areas, so that presently I should see cavalry or armoured cars dash across the rolling countryside to stop the train. Hope clung to me through Bohain and Busigny on to Le Cateau – had not British troops fought there? There might yet be survivors, stragglers cut off from the Retreat, hidden among the friendly woods and villages of this last corner of France ... The express train rushed on. The sort of 'something' which I so wanted to happen did not occur. It seldom does.

'You can still see the trenches the English dug on the hills to the west,' said the German officer who accompanied me, as we steamed through Le Cateau. 'And in the town I have been shown the house and the very bed in which your British General slept.'

It gave me a pang of loneliness to see the place, silent and at peace in the wintry sunshine, whence my own people had so long departed. They had fought there and retreated; I wanted to follow them, to get back beyond the lines – before it was too late, before I left France. It seemed to me that if I could get away now I would be able to go straight back to the Squadron without let or hindrance, that I would be reinstated in my cabin in the barge and allowed to fly again. Even the Major would be pleased to see me. I should get a new machine and be able to carry on as if nothing had happened. Otherwise – if I delayed – it might be weeks, months before I could get back by some means as yet unknown to me. And then only to England. 'They' might not let me go back to France ...

At dusk we crossed the Belgian frontier.

'Do we pass through Mons?' I asked.

'Mons?'

'Yes, where a battle was fought in the early days – the first battle in which the English were engaged.'

'Never heard of it,' was the answer. And at that the war, active operations at all events, became suddenly immeasurably distant ...

We passed Liege – its German name, Lüttich, plastered everywhere for they meant to keep it – and then just beyond, still in Belgium and close now to Holland, the train came to a standstill. A dark night, damp and misty. My heart began to thump unpleasantly. Holland meant salvation, people came back from Holland. Now or never? There were four men with rifles in the carriage, tough fellows from the front who would stand no nonsense and could presumably shoot straight, and an officer with an automatic pistol. How could anything be done? I heard my voice tremble as I asked to go to the lavatory.

They watched the windows as I went, they lined the corridor. Two men came with me, one wedged his foot in the lavatory door. I could have kicked the foot away, but I could not have opened and got out of the window in time. And I hadn't a map or a compass, or so much as a penny-piece with which to buy protection. I thought of the advice given me by a Frenchman in St Quentin gaol, to wait until I could procure essential equipment in some camp in Germany. I had told him that I believed my own nose to be sufficient equipment, that judging from the goal we were in I could smell my way to freedom.

'*Mais il faut tout de meme vue boussole!*' he had protested. And when I found that I could not get out of the lavatory window I consoled myself by thinking that he was probably right.

The train moved on again. Presently we came to the German frontier, and so to Cologne. A long wait in the cold, a still longer journey in a slow train up the Rhine valley, and at dawn – the citadel of Mainz.

Mainz, where I first learnt at close quarters of Escape, and where I spent my first Christmas in captivity ...

'It's all very well for you,' a Mons prisoner told me. 'This is only your first – for me it's the second, and God knows where we'll spend next Christmas.'

I laughed at him. Another Christmas here in Germany? Impossible! I had to get back. We all had to get back.

'Do you *really* think it will be over by the end of next year?'

It's funny how I remember that question and the rather despairing voice in which it was put – funny because the speaker was to escape and be killed before the end of the war, and also because one does not generally remember the foolish answers one has given.

'Of course it will be over!' I asserted with all the ignorance which, in newly-captured prisoners, passed for expert knowledge. 'Think of the Blockade and of the new Armies in England!'

'Think of Serbia. Think of the Dardanelles!'

'Oh, they'll soon be forgotten! Why, our offensive next summer will drive the Boche right back into Germany.'

'I hope you're right,' he answered soberly. And then he looked at his wrist-watch and sighed: 'It's 10 o'clock, Thursday, and we're still in prison.'

And we were still in prison, though in different camps, when summer came and the soft west wind brought us a faint mutter of guns.

*   *   *

I first heard the guns at Weilburg, towards the end of February in 1916. I was very depressed at the time because the tunnel we had been digging had caved in and all our other schemes for escape seemed slowly to be coming to a ruinous end. After the tunnel failure there had been a sudden and thorough search for contraband by the authorities. In my room we had had scarcely any warning and some of our most precious possessions were pounced upon before we had time to do anything.

The day previously I had been hammering out a passable imitation of a German *laissez-passer* on a borrowed typewriter, and several copies had not yet been securely hidden. I grabbed mine almost from under a German hand and crammed it into a large German pipe which was to form part of my disguise when I should at length manage to escape. A couple of hundred marks of German paper money (contraband of course) went into the bowl on top of the forged pass, and finally a thick wad of tobacco, tightly pressed down. As the Germans, going systematically from bed to bed, began to search my scant belongings I stuck the pipe between my teeth and lit a match.

Now I hate a pipe. The beastly thing always burns my tongue, uses up all my matches, gurgles and makes a most unpleasant smell. I never smoke one. And the result, on this occasion, was that I did not know how to handle it. I managed to make it draw, in spite of the pass and the paper money – in fact, it drew so well that unless the Germans left quickly I ran the risk of swallowing some 200 marks' worth of smoke – but, instead of holding it by the bowl and waving it about in the carefree manner pipe-smokers have, I clung firmly to the stem with my teeth.

The searchers finished the bed-to-bed inspection and began to look over the prisoners individually. It was not a very thorough 'frisking,' but the officer in charge was sharp-eyed and no fool. All at once I got a dig in the ribs from the prisoner next to me.

'Look out, man! Take that pipe out of your mouth – quick!'

I squinted down at the bowl to see what was wrong. It had gone out, I was glad to note, leaving a nice grey ash above my buried treasure, but it was certainly behaving in a most peculiar manner. It was bobbing up and down like a piston rod-vibrating, trembling ... My teeth were chattering!

The authorities noticed nothing, but I nearly threw the damned pipe out of the window then and there, and when the search was over I went disconsolately out to the parade ground to consider my stupidity. More than stupidity, it was unwarrantable nervousness. If I were going to tremble and let my teeth chatter at nothing more exciting than a search, what would happen when it came to escaping? Could I hope to walk past a sentry nonchalantly, or through a village of staring Germans? How would I behave at the crucial moment, either getting out of the camp or on the frontier? I began to think that perhaps I was no good at the game, or rather – for I hated to admit so much – that continual thinking about getting back had made me nervous and easily excited.

Anyhow, I was depressed and worried, walking round the parade ground, I fell in with a Frenchman depressed and worried about Verdun. He was a good fellow, this Frenchman, and keen on escape. When walking he had an odd habit of inserting his hand between shirt and trousers to scratch himself violently between the legs. Occasionally he would remove the hand in order to pick his nose, but the fact that he did it with his little finger seemed to give the action a certain courtly grace. I told him of the search, of my frantic desire to get out and back to France, of my hopes and of my fears of failure. He shrugged his shoulders, told me not to worry and quoted some common-place maxim – of Napoleon's, or was it La Rochefoucauld's? – to prove that ultimate success was a matter of perse-verance. Then, in the farthest comer of the camp, he suddenly seized my arm.

'Listen!' he said.

I listened and heard the swish of water. The River Lahn ran close to the camp boundary. About 100 yards downstream was a weir over which the water splashed with a gentle, persistent murmur. But it was not to that the Frenchman bade me listen. I faced about. Half a mile away a train rumbled over a bridge and into a tunnel – a *Schnellzug* from Giessen, via Limburg, to the Rhine. I often watched the trains, they might be of use to an escaping prisoner. But still my French friend was not satisfied. He raised his hand. I looked up, held my breath, listened more intently.

Weilburg camp lay in the valley. Steep wooded slopes rose upon either side of the winding Lahn. It was a calm day, the trees stood gaunt and still. In the upper air just the least drift from the west … Something moved in my ears, a slight increase of pressure, a softened shock upon my cheek. I glanced around, wondering whether I had actually heard anything. The silence increased. The train had gone, and I could scarcely hear the river now. What wind there had been, dropped altogether. A nearby sentry clanked his rifle, and stood motionless. And then it struck me that the whole world was listening – the hills, the very trees, the water in the stream. Suddenly, I heard.

It was scarcely a sound; if it could be compared to anything it was perhaps most like a distant and exceedingly deep-throated growl. But one could feel the concussion more than hear the sound, it was as if the earth itself had shuddered, and as I listened with raised head I swear that I saw the branches of a tree tremble ever so slight. The world was apprehensive.

'That,' said my Frenchman in an awed tone, 'is Verdun. The Boche artillery is busy – generally we only hear it at night. They are making a big effort to break through.'

'*Mais ils ne passeront pas!*' he added hurriedly. That night the west wind blew strongly, driving snowclouds before it, whistling through ill-fitting doors and windows. In between the gusts we heard the cannonade clearly, echoing over the valley. It seemed closer now, a definite sound rather than a concussion – and not 200 miles away but 20! Verdun was going through its long agony. Verdun–Champagne–Picardy–Artois!

It was exasperating. I wanted to leave the camp that night …

'*Attendez-donc le printemps,*' counselled the Frenchman.

*   *   *

There were some who said that they heard the guns of the Somme battle from the camp of Friedber, which is near Bad Nauheim. But I did not hear them myself until one autumn day when I rested upon a hillside in the Taunus forest.

It was 25 September, the day – if I remember rightly – of the taking of Mouquet Farm. Or was it of some deadly assault upon Thiepval? Without referring to military histories I cannot be certain; but I do know that it was an important day upon the battlefields in Picardy as in Hessen. For as to the latter region three of us had just escaped. And though our victory was doomed to be as ephemeral as that upon the Somme – or indeed as that at Loos, a year previously to the day – yet it was an exceptional occasion, a landmark upon the road to ultimate success.

We had walked out of the camp in German uniform of our own making, we had bluffed our way past stolid German sentries, feeling like the immortal Mr Toad – with the soldiers all saluting as we marched along the road – and we were free.

At the crucial moments – and there had been many – my nerves had stood the test. I had trembled less than on the day when the pipe was between my teeth. My heart was thumping heavily, but with exertion as much as with excitement for the sun at noon had become unpleasantly hot and I was wearing civilian clothing under my German disguise, not to mention several pounds weight of provisions tightly secured to my body. The last mile or two across open country had been very trying, so many suspicious eyes had been fixed upon us; the population of this normally quiet part of the world seemed all at once to have multiplied in an alarming fashion. The woods by contrast were still and deserted. The shade, the silence, the soft grass and thick protective undergrowth tempted us to stop, but the thought of pursuit, of those suspicious German eyes in the fields and along the roads, urged us on. The third man of our party was 'going home' by a different route; we parted from him at the foot of the hill and climbed hurriedly through the trees.

Once when we sat down for a moment's rest we heard shots and imagined a hue and a cry after our unfortunate companion. We marched on, faster than before, up the steepest slope into the densest part of the woods.

At length we halted, panting for breath. My ears were singing, a fly buzzed in my face, my heart pounded; a drop of perspiration ran down my forehead, splashed on my hand. But the forest was silent. Just the faint sounds of late summer: a little tune whistled by a bird, the rustling of a leaf, some very small animal moving stealthily through some dead leaves, and the distant creaking of a farm cart. We were safe from pursuit. Discarding heavy overcoats we sat down to rest.

Through the branches of the trees we looked out, so steep was the hill, over the wide and rolling Hessian plain. A peaceful scene for others than ourselves to gaze upon; for us the peace was treacherous, lulling us to false security. In that plain stood Friedberg and its prison, men hurried along the roads or lurked in the villages seeking our recapture. We could rest now in safety, but that night we must be on our way, come down from the hills, cross the plain. It was our battlefield; the fight was on. We had to get back ... And from over our shoulders as we faced the plain came the reminder of that deadlier battlefield to which we were striving to return. There was no mistaking it – the thunder of the thousand guns.

I call it thunder for want of a better word, because in reality it was not like a thunderstorm at all. A thunderstorm rings the changes; it comes from one point, then from another; it comes nearer rapidly or dies away altogether; it rolls and echoes, the end of a peal sometimes louder than the beginning. There was nothing of that sort in what we heard. It came from one direction only and was almost continuous, constant in volume; sometimes a little louder perhaps, but always on the same strangely deep note. It seemed to come out of the earth like a groan from the hills. And again I noticed, or thought I did, that when the sound was loudest the trees trembled, and I am sure I felt a sort of vibrating pressure upon my face and ears. It seemed to come in waves. There was no distinguishing between isolated shots or groups of shots, what we heard was the voice of all the guns raised in one great muffled roar. A moving, an affecting sound. It gave me a feeling half-way between anger and fear. But when I looked out over the plain what I felt principally was hope. Hope that I would soon be seeing – from the air! – what I heard beneath the trees.

'March to the sound of the guns!'

Napoleon may or may not have said that, but he would certainly not have practised it had he stood in our shoes upon the Taunus. He would have done what we did, turned his back on that distant battle and marched across the peaceful-looking plain. To the south, and to Switzerland! That night we came down from the sheltering hillside and fought our battle with map and compass against wakeful farms and villages, and men on bicycles or on foot with police dogs, and telephones and motor cars ...

On the fifth day we lost the battle, and when we were taken back to Friedberg it was raining and we could no longer hear the guns on the Somme.

*   *   *

It was a long time before I heard them again after that. One certainly could not hear them in Fort Zorndorf or in the gaol of Cüstrin. If Allied artillery ever had been heard there, as I was told by a sanguine Russian it had, then the guns had long since been silenced and now lay rusting in the

Masurian Lakes. No encouraging sounds were likely to be heard again from that edge of the map.

And yet we did hear them. I'm sure of it. How else did we keep our hearts beating through that depressing winter, how else but with the certainty that we should get back before the end? Before the end – that was the trouble. It seemed impossible for the war to go on much longer, not beyond the next summer offensive which this time must be successful. We prayed for victory and for an end to the war; yes, but we prayed more devoutly for the means to get back, free. The fear of not getting back in time was growing stronger, and I was not the only one to feel it.

There were prisoners – though not many in Fort Zorndorf – who either had never thought of escape or else had given it up as a bad job. They learnt languages from French or Russian prisoners, which may possibly have helped them after the war, but principally they collected odds and ends of clothing, books, furniture, and nicknackery. Some of them knitted to pass the time, others – perhaps in revenge for their own captivity – kept birds in cages. To those of us who hoped against hope that we would get back before the end, the sight of these assorted trophies, the *lares et penates* of a war spent in stagnation, was more horrible than pink rats to a man with DTs.

'If I can't escape I would sooner get a sentry to shoot me dead than travel home at the end of the war with the canaries and the knitting!'

That was the way H— expressed it one day as we walked furiously around the ramparts of the fort, and I'm sure that he meant it. At the time it even seemed possible that he would have to put his threat into execution, for we appeared to be much further from freedom than from the end of the war. But, looking back, I can see that it was written that he should never take a seat in the 'Canary Cage Express', and so I can understand why he so often repeated in our most downcast moments of failure – 'I *know* we shall get back – I *know* it!'

There were other, brighter days when we confidently believed that our sails had caught the wind of Fortune. I remember some brave words, and thoughts too, at about Christmas-time – my second in captivity – for in the first days of January H— and I were due to escape. In silence we drank to success. But the wine must have been polluted.

We were out for one wild night and part of a day. Recaptured just as we were gaining confidence. Gaoled in Cüstrin. Back to Fort Zorndorf. Out again in February. Gaoled for dreary months in Cüstrin – while the Germans fell back on the Hindenburg Line, while the Czar abdicated, while the Americans came feebly and belatedly into the war, while the French fell back in disorder from the Aisne – then back to the inexpugnable Fort. Not finally discouraged – Zorndorf was never Doubting Castle – but fearful of the end. No use sitting back doing nothing, no use waiting for unmerited luck – like a certain amiable Frenchman who used frequently to visit our room.

'Oh, yes, I shall escape someday,' he would repeat complacently. 'Some day they will take me close to the Dutch frontier and then it will be easy. There is a part of the frontier which I know from before the war – some Dutch friends of mine live on the other side – near Enschede.' He pronounced it 'N's-K-T.' He was very fat and took his name from the greatest of Bysantine Emperors – if he resembled him in character then I am no longer surprised at the Decline and Fall. But in appearance he bore a strong resemblance to the German Commandant, so strong that we saw in it a means to escape. Before going any further with the plans, we approached the Emperor.

'Would you like to escape?'

'Yes, and what is more I shall escape. When I get to N's-K-T—'

'Yes, yes, but that's a long way off. How about getting a little closer?'

'Certainly – a good idea. I think the Boches will be taking me there shortly. They cannot keep me in this Fort much longer. Now, near N's-K-T there is —'

'Maybe, but suppose we start by getting out of the camp. What would you say if we made you a nice German uniform and you took us for a little stroll past the sentries and out of the main gate?'

'*Quoi*? Disguise me as a *sale Boche*?' exclaimed the horrified Emperor. '*Ah – non alors, jamais!* Besides, it is too risky. I prefer to wait until I get to N's-K-T.' And for all I know he may be waiting yet. No, it was hopeless to sit still, wishing but sinking inactively into the Slough of Despond. No use, on the other hand, dashing off without plan, purpose or equipment just for the sake of being at large for a few uncomfortable hours or days. Perseverance alone was not enough – witness the two Russian soldiers.

They came bedraggled, footsore, half-starved into the Citadel of Cüstrin. They had no kit at all, other than the rags they stood in. They had been employed by their captors at putting up barbed-wire fencing somewhere, a long way off, in the west. The sun set in the west, they knew that, and it rose in the east, over Holy Russia. Eastward ho! they marched. They marched for forty-five days. When they gave themselves up exhausted, they could just remember the name of the place from which they had started. The Germans laughed. The place was on the Dutch frontier!

Perhaps it was N's-K-T.

With such examples before us and with the ever-growing fear of failure in our hearts, we were anxious not to throw away chances in ignorance or folly. Folly? It might be coming to that. There were crazy ones in every camp. In Fort Zorndorf they seemed to become daily more numerous, and I think H— would agree with me that at times we were all a bit light-headed. The intense desire for liberty, the gnawing fear of canaries in cages and of a train home after the war, the seclusion, the close contact with other men – of other nationalities, of one's own nationality, I don't know which was worse – the smells and the habits of some, the harmless mannerisms magnified into vices of others, drunkenness and Russian pessimism, the gloom and dank discomfort of the Fort – these things made violent rage seem the natural relief from an intolerable and unnatural existence. But just as bodily disease calls forth inner powers of defence, so did fear stimulate the flow of a necessary serum – the increasing determination to succeed, the concentration upon escape amounting to an *idee fixe*. We seldom thought of anything else.

No, we never heard the guns in Fort Zorndorf, and I am glad we did not. The sound added to those we already heard in our heads would have driven us frantic.

*   *   *

I think Strindberg might have enjoyed prison life: no women. *Per contra* – there were cats (*felis 'vulgaris' malodorous*) and kittens of all colours and conditions. Some misguided individual had, in the early days of the war, brought a couple of the brutes into Fort Zorndorf and, like rabbits in Australia, they were good at multiplication. Several prisoners, doubtless mentally enfeebled, kept packs of them.

One Frenchman – a cavalry officer at that – possessed a dozen or so which he had reared from infancy and for whom he had constructed an elaborate runway from his window so that they could be put out at nights. His favourite puss answered to the name of 'Taupiné'. Alas, during the hard winter months the cats vanished one by one, until at length only Taupiné remained. A fat little thing with blue eyes and a snug coat like moleskin. One day a wandering prisoner heard sounds of singing coming from the French cavalryman's room. He peered through the door. The cavalryman in white apron and forage cap was stirring a big stewpot. Pinned to the wall by the four corners like some trophy of an African shoot was a small furry skin. And the song he sang was, '*Lorsque tout est fini* ...' Poor Taupiné, they tell me she made excellent eating.

But caterwauling was not the only music we heard. Russian songs were not then so hackneyed as now and the sadder the Russian the better the singing. Some of them might be half-seas-over for the greater part of each day, but they could always manage to sing or play a guitar at night. They harmonised, they improvised, they had music in their souls – too much music, it reduced their characters to a matter of fugues and subterfuge. The French knew better how to treat their music in those dark days of prison life. They might be fiercely patriotic at times, quaintly vulgar at others, but they were invariably light-hearted in their singing – in addition to being ready at all times to annoy their captors by such heartless teasing as would have made the very saints in heaven crack their haloes with rage. We had many a laugh with the French, but I can also remember lying very still in bed on certain nights at Fort Zorndorf, listening to Roland Garros in the next room play his violin. It was winter, and he played well ... I was glad when later he escaped, even though it was but to be killed in France. He was another for whom it was written that he should not return with the knitting, the cats and the caged birds.

However, such music as we heard in the dismal rooms and passages of the Fort never drowned the fancied thunder of the guns, nor made me forget that more thrilling music of the wind in the wires. But as time wore on I realised that a change had come over my ideas of 'getting back'. In fact, I perceived that it was no longer 'back', but 'on' for which I must strive. I began secretly to doubt whether I should be able to handle an aeroplane with any degree of safety. Conditions had so changed that the wings upon my tunic seemed more of a reproach than an emblem of my capacity as a pilot; I would in any case be hopelessly out of date. No question of returning quietly, unobstrusively to the Squadron on the Lys – even if it were still stationed there – the machines had changed, so had their engines, their armaments, the very quality of the pilots. A new gener-ation of airmen had grown up in France, a generation practised in the art of aerial fighting in which evolutions that went far beyond anything we had dreamed of in 1915 were performed daily and as a matter of course. Why, they not only knew how to get out of a spin, they were taught how to get into one!

The German press sang the praises of airmen whose victories were numbered by the score; the French acclaimed as 'aces' their heroes of a dozen combats. The British *communiqués* alone divulged no names – and rightly so – but newly captured prisoners brought the news.

'The BE 2c?' gasped one whose accent made me think of plump brown birds clucking in the heather. 'Och-man, she's been dead these twelve months an' more! Maybe, there's a '2e' left yet, but I doobt it.'

And he went on to tell me of single-seater machines – whole squadrons of them! – whose top speed was over 100 miles an hour, whose guns fired through the propeller, whose pilots flew and fought in formation and were experts in 'stunting' of an incredible sort.

'The Germans have Richthofen and Boelcke,' I said. 'And the French have Guynemer. Tell me who stands for our side?'

'Well – there's a lot o' young fellows disputing the honours. Some o' them have thirty or more Huns to their names. But I'd say the greatest o' the whole crowd is – Captain Ball …'

I did not forget that name.

More than thirty successful fights! I looked ruefully down at my Wings. They had faded and shrunk in the course of captivity, and the day at Gosport when I had proudly watched them being sewn on to my tunic was very far away. At twenty I seemed already to be old, useless, discarded, a survivor from some harmless little campaign of the past.

* * *

If from the camp of Strohem Moor we did not actually hear the bombardment at Ypres, at least we had the illusion of being close to the front. The country was flat, desolate, intersected by marshy streams. Holland seemed much less than 100 miles away – 'little' Holland, 'little' Belgium and then the old, the haunting, the glorious wretchedness of Flanders. The very camp – with its wire and machine-gun towers, its débris, its newly captured prisoners, its flies and its ill-health – resembled the cages where captives were herded in war zones. There was, too, a new restlessness among the prisoners, born of ill-treatment, of discontent and of long inactivity. Never had so many prisoners wanted to escape – wanted, tried, in some cases succeeded! It was no longer any use for the Germans to attempt by friendly means to discourage us. No good for the more tactful of our enemies to smile and say: 'It is impossible! You see? – so-and-so has been recaptured, and somebody else has been caught on the frontier. *Es ist unmoglich. Uber die Grenze kommen Sie nie!'*

We knew well enough that it was possible. The only question was *when* … The Russian collapse appeared to have postponed the end, yet victory in the west seemed imminent. For what else did we go on hammering at Poelkappelle and Langemark and Passchendaele than for a decisive victory by the end of the year? Was there still a chance to get back, a chance to learn to fly again, to strike a blow before it was all over – or perhaps before all nations met with catastrophe?

Catastrophe! *Dies irae* of the western world! It began to look like that when autumn closed in with rain and mist to droop our spirits over the bad news … The U-boats were terrible, and the victory of Passchendaele was losing us the war. The French were scarcely fighting save amongst themselves; the German people were desperate, half-starving and with bitter talk in the land; but the Americans were slower than even a giant has the right to be. Holy Russia was dead. For a moment Cambrai lit up the darkness with a flash bright as a calcium flare, then the inky blackness of Caporetto climaxed the year's disasters.

Prisoners escaped, but more were taken. I listened awe-struck to fresh tales of France. A changed France! And a changed warfare, on land as in the air. With none of it could I claim to be familiar. The Wings were shrivelled on my breast. And still hope persisted, and the abominable fear of not returning, of not succeeding, of being a Knitting-and-Canary man, spurred us on. For me, it was in and out of the wire, in and out of gaol, in and out of hospital, finally into gaol and off to the Saar district.

My third Christmas in captivity was spent at Neunkirchen.

* * *

We heard the guns from that place all right. Night and day, as often as not. And not only field-guns from the French front, but, by the irony of chance, guns of the same category with which once – how long ago! – I had been on intimate terms. 'Archie!' The Allied raiders were busy over the Saar.

And once more the guns put new strength into our determination. They thudded in time to our obstinate tunnel digging. They pounded away despair when the tunnel was discovered. They hammered fresh and ever more ingenious ideas into our heads. They fired a salvo to salute the luck which transferred me to Aachen ...

'The war will be over in six weeks from now,' a German informed me after 21st March. 'Either we win, or else, we have shot our bolt ...'

The end was coming. Where was my hope of flying now?

'I've just heard from my brother,' I was told by a young pilot, my accomplice in escaping at the time, 'that's he's flying all the latest machines. Some of them do 140! Lucky devil – I'm afraid we shall get back too late.' But he need not have worried. He was another of those destined to escape and die before the end. However, he would have been just as keen had he known about it ...

Aachen! By all that's wonderful, they took me there of their own free will – although against mine, for I had protested, warned them. I would not go to a camp whence people were shipped off in Holland to await the end of the war in permanent inescapable captivity, albeit in comfort. I would stay in Germany and I would escape. With comical insistence they took me to Aachen. Just for one night. But it was enough for two of us.

We looked out of an upper-story window in the camp building and saw a blurred ridge of hills that must lie in Holland. In Holland! I had not been so close to the frontier for more than two years – not since the night in December, 1915, when I had peered from the lavatory of a railway carriage. And now, mid-April, 1918, I escaped through a lavatory ventilator, into another lavatory, out through a lavatory drain. The incessant repetition of the word is still painful to me; but, although it is a sad thing when one's road through the Valley of Humiliation is lined with sanitary appliances, it seems to have been written as a part of my fate ...

We tramped through the night and upon the following morning, at breakfast in Holland, I first heard the momentous question:

'What are you going to do next?'

Before starting from Aachen I had cut the old Wings from my tattered tunic. I knew now that I would soon be able to get a new pair.

* * *

I cannot for a moment pretend that all, or indeed any, of those thoughts 'flashed' through my head whilst I answered His Majesty's questions. But all of them and many more – memories of long periods of solitary confinement, reminiscences of escapes of mine and of others – were lodged in that mysterious locality known as the back of one's mind. And in the effort to extract events necessary to make a brief and coherent story, I found that the whole lot had come willy-nilly to the surface.

With the result that when, at the end of the interview, I tiptoed down silent, red-carpeted corridors, I began to wonder whether I should be able to escape from the Palace. The past which I had evoked was not so easily shaken off. Mental habits, grafted on during two years and a half of captivity, reasserted themselves so that when I stepped out into the sunlight I was overwhelmed by fears similar to those of Friedberg. I wanted to feel in my pockets to see if map, compass, money and forged pass were safe. I would have liked, but scarcely dared, to pull the cap down over my eyes, for a policeman on the gate watched me suspiciously and I fancied the sentry, halted by his box, was squinting through the little hole at the side. Anxiously I went over the precepts of escaping in daylight and through the main gate: Don't walk too fast; don't be too stiff; look about you as though you owned the place; swing your arms naturally, not as if you were half-strangled by the strings holding your kit together; don't forget to answer salutes; and remember to say a few words of the language within hearing of the sentry... I stumbled on, breathing heavily. I came to the gate. The sentry had marched off, but already he was at the end of his beat, was turning, was about to come back. He would reach the gate at the same time as I passed through it. I dreaded meeting him, he looked fierce and horribly wide-awake ... All at once I heard a thudding sound. It was the policeman coming to attention. I gazed at him benignly, answered his salute in a leisurely manner and said, 'Good morning, Sergeant,' loud enough for the sentry to hear. He was halted now, standing at ease, but he heard me speak – it was my talking *English* that did it! – sprang to attention, slo-o-oped Hipe, and smacked the butt of his rifle smartly with the fingers of his right hand.

I think I grinned, I may even have waved, but I certainly sighed with relief as I marched on past the crowd of gaping idlers. I was out of the camp – er – palace, and no one, not even the policeman, had seen that I was merely an escaped prisoner masquerading as an air-pilot.

*   *   *

After that, thinking it well to strike while the iron was hot, I went straight to the Air Ministry and told the Director of Something-or-Other that the King had said I might go out to the front as soon as I chose.

I had not expected that my statement would be believed, and I don't suppose that it was, but it certainly had some effect. A benevolent staff gentleman, dressed in pale blue and covered from head to foot in gold braid, smiled '... and took a perfectly enormous book.'

I have no idea what it was called, but it looked like a ledger and the gentleman's manner was that of an obliging salesman. The conversation as I recall it was something like this:

The Gentleman: 'Want to go back to the front, do you? H'm – a rather unusual order, if I may say so. Well, let me see – we have a nice selection of fronts. There's Salonika – that might suit you ...'

Self: 'Er – France ...'

Gentleman (imperturbably): 'And then there's Palestine. Quite a demand for Palestine these days – nice climate ...'

Self: 'But I don't want ...'

Gentleman: 'Of course, we could always let you have Africa.' (He spoke as if he were giving me the whole continent.) 'It's quiet there now, but more pilots are needed – nice sea journey and ... '

Self (loudly): 'I want to go to France!'

The Gentleman looked at me in a pained way.

'France?' he repeated as though he had never heard of it. 'Oh, I'm afraid we couldn't do that. We have no authority.'

Self: 'But why not? I flew in France before, I was captured there and ...'

Gentleman: 'That's just it. You might be captured again!'

He sighed and closed the ledger, sorry not to have been able to book an order.

I tried another room in the Air Ministry.

Here a much more understanding person told me, after listening to my tale of woe, that he thought it could be arranged. The trouble was that hitherto no one captured flying in France had been allowed to return to fly in France, because – and I had to admit the truth of this – capture was one of the most likely things to happen to an air-pilot. And apart from the vague possibility of an officer, captured for the second time, being an enemy agent, there was the more serious probability of his being harshly treated by the Germans. Personally I thought that the likelihood of being recognised on capture would be exceedingly remote, and afterwards – but, touching wood, I had no intention of being recaptured.

'It may happen, however,' my friend insisted, 'and therefore it will be best if you adopt another name when you get to the front.'

'When I get to the front! But how am I to get there?'

'Well – I think if you go back to your Training Squadron, pass through the tests and the various courses, and say nothing, the Air Ministry will forget about you in time. Then, when a batch of pilots is sent out to France, your name won't be noticed amongst the others. And I promise you my department will make no objections.'

I took him at his word and returned to London Colne where I had been posted shortly after landing in England. I had taken no leave, for I knew that I could always get occasional days and weekends off while learning to fly. There was plenty of time, I thought, for me to get back to the front. The great German attack was held up; there would be a return push in the summer, driving on through the winter; and next spring, with the Americans properly in the field at last, the final battles would be fought. The war would last for another year. I curbed my impatience and took up the 'new' flying with enthusiasm.

But it was not so easy to 'say nothing'. It soon got about that I was an escaped prisoner and, although a lot of people did not quite know what this meant, everyone was more or less interested. A paragraph in the Press, my audience with the King, the fact that I had already flown in France stimulated the interest of the bluff and rubicund Commanding Officer. He was for ever asking, 'What are you going to do now?' and showing that he was only too willing to help me. Unfortunately his help was applied in the wrong direction. I could have had a seat in his office for the asking – and Lord knows to what dizzy heights that might not have led me – a position on the Wing Staff, or perhaps even gold braid and the Air

Ministry. So many people wished me well, and their repeated offers of employment were sometimes very tempting.

'They're short of a Flight Commander in one of the Home Defence squadrons,' I was told one day, for the suggestions were not always for ground jobs. 'That ought to be in your line – shoot down all the Huns who come over London.'

I declined with thanks. The menace of air raids was beginning to dwindle; besides, my mind was set upon other raids in France.

A greater danger faced me whilst the Commanding Officer was away on leave, when a young but remarkably offensive Flight Commander took temporary charge of the Squadron office. I went in there one morning, for the simple formality of requesting permission to dine in London that night, and rather to my surprise was summoned to the inner sanctum.

'So you want to go up to town, do you?' the temporary CO snarled, his tone reminding me of Growl in the far-off days upon the Lys. But I was not impressed. This young lad had not seen what I had seen; he must have been at school when I was taken prisoner.

'Well, you can't go,' he went on. 'You've already been there three or four times this week. Much too much. Can't stand that sort of thing – setting a bad example to the junior officers. You ought to be farther away from London. I'm putting down your name on the instructors' list. You'll be sent off to do the course in instruction ...'

An instructor! The last thing I wanted to be; I foresaw trouble ... But no further unpleasantness came from that quarter – the young Flight Commander was killed on the following day, trying, I'm afraid, to show off on a new type of single-seater. With his most regrettable end I thought selfishly enough that the last obstacle had fallen.

But when the Major returned from leave he brought the rumoured news that I was to be sent with a party of other pilots to hunt German submarines off the Scilly Islands.

The Scilly Islands! No doubt it was war work, and important work at that. Yet it was not to flutter feebly over the Atlantic that I had taken the trouble to escape.

... *Had* I escaped? I began to doubt it. I seemed to be surrounded by a network of obstacles.

The officials at the Air Ministry were as hard to deal with as German camp-commandants, some of my brother officers at the Training Squadron as unsympathetic as Landsturm guards. And I did not at first feel at home amongst the younger pilots and pupils. They were a very different lot from those of my early flying days, and the spirit was not the same. Not that either the spirit or indeed the pilots themselves were any worse; on the contrary, in spite of the extreme youth of the majority, they were a good lot and keen as mustard, especially the young Americans of whom there were now a large number at every station. But there was a sort of devil-may-care, hard-drinking recklessness about them all that made them careless in an equal degree of, say, the risks of flying or of signing a blank cheque. Life was short, they were going to have a good time before it ended and damn the expense. The casualties in flying training establishments were heavy.

It was a long job, but – thank heavens! – I never lost sight of the end in view. Slowly I passed through the usual business of engine-fitting, rigging, machine-gunnery, and graduation from the Avro to the Sopwith 'Pup', from the 'Pup' to the Spad, finally to the SE 5. I was shown all the mysteries of aerobatics and taught – very badly – how to fly in formation. At length, in August, I was ready. The Air Ministry said nothing; 'they' seemed to have forgotten all about me. Young pilots who had started their training just before me began to move overseas. Only the shortage of SE 5 practice machines held me up until the middle of the month.

And then one morning orders came for me to join a School of Aerial Fighting in Yorkshire.

*   *   *

There was something very puzzling about this posting to Yorkshire. It was not absolutely essential for a pilot, especially for one who had been to France before, to pass through an Aerial Fighting School; to my own knowledge several fledgelings had gone direct from the Training Squadron to France. I had now all the necessary qualifications in flying, gunnery and so on, and my friend at the Air Ministry had kept his word about letting my name through in the ordinary way, without mention of capture or escape. Why, therefore, had I of all others been selected to go so far north as Yorkshire? A Fighting School was, of course, another step on the way to the front, but it was also another delay. I began to see in this move the action of some well-meaning but misguided individual at the Air Ministry, someone who saw that by sending me to Yorkshire a little more time would be gained, another chance that I might change my mind. After the course of fighting instruction there were other stations to which 'they' might send me; 'Home Defence' loomed menacingly near.

With these uneasy suspicions in mind I kept my eyes open as soon as I stepped into the Headquarters office of the Fighting School. I don't quite know what I expected to find, but I wandered around trying to look innocent in much the same way as I had in the past hunted for valuable loot in some German *Kommandantur*. Presently my name amongst others was called out by one of the staff, and on hearing it a clerk rose from a corner of the room, crossed over and handed me a small bundle of papers.

I glanced through them. There were a couple of letters forwarded to me by the Air Ministry, a claim for some allowance or other, and an open envelope with my name in one corner and the Commanding Officer's in the other. An envelope which at once increased my suspicions and my fears of interference. I turned it over in my hands: what was it?– a sort of letter of introduction? In that case the open flap and my name in the corner gave me a right to read it ... Dodging behind the line of waiting pilots, I opened it and read.

When I came to the end I fancy I must have smiled at the luck which had allowed this letter to fall into my hands before it reached the CO. It was from a fairly highly placed and influential friend of mine at the Air Ministry. It contained a glowing account of my captivity and escape, and expressed the writer's hope that I should be treated rather differently from the average brand-new pilot at the School, that perhaps a job could be found for me on the staff, at any rate temporarily – until a vacancy occurred on the *Italian* front! The letter concluded with the statement that, whereas I was anxious to proceed overseas, it was considered undesirable that I should return to France ...

In the days of my captivity I had learnt that on recapture, after an attempted escape, the first thing to do was to destroy efficiently the maps and other incriminating documents one was carrying. Months of concentration upon the one subject of escape had brought such lessons in habit up to the level of instinct. In this office of the School on the distant Yorkshire coast, seeing that I was in danger of recapture, the instinct asserted itself. I tore the envelope and the letter to small pieces which I distributed carefully among several wastepaper baskets ... It was not for nothing that my Wings had been sewn on in the heyday of the Longhorn, and no one in that gathering of newly-fledged pilots realised that I was escaping again.

Two days later, the School being greatly overcrowded, it was decided to send away a batch of those pilots who had some previous tuition in aerial fighting and sufficient flying-hours to their credit. The majority of these pilots were young Colonials and Americans serving in the British forces, light-hearted, keen for adventure in the air, elated that their stay in Yorkshire had been cut short. They left the School singing and cheering happily, for their orders were to report at the Air Ministry on their way to France. And I can testify that they sang and cheered and were happy, because it happened that I was one of them.

*   *   *

I had no idea of the intricate organisation which had grown up for the disposal of pilots in France. I had imagined that, as on a previous occasion, I would have to wander about looking for a headquarters or an office of sorts, that I might have difficulty in finding any one who cared a damn where I went to or when, but that by the end of twenty-four hours I should somehow have drifted off to a squadron, and that there the fun would begin at once.

It wasn't at all like that. The number of officials at Boulogne surprised me; it seemed dismally certain that the Army in France had been over-taken by efficiency. They were like ushers in a movie theatre, inspecting your seat tickets before letting you through to the performance. And as in a theatre, so here there were clear distinctions between tickets of different value. Staff ticket-holders were led off at once to the royal box; Generals to the dress-circle; Colonels, Majors and such packed into cars and driven away to the stalls; while subalterns and other ranks crammed into the same old tumble-down trains which would eventually deposit them within walking distance of the pit. As for air-pilots, the ushers did not appear to like them at all. We were the cheap seats. But instead of allowing us to go straight up to the gallery, they pushed us into a train that steamed off in the wrong direction – away from the front!

It was not until we had passed Etaples and were almost at Berck that I understood we were going to a sort of livestock depot known as a 'Pilots' Pool'. We arrived late at night and I could neither see nor discover anything of the place until the following morning. Then to my horror I found that I was back in prison . . . We lived and messed in huts like those at Ströhen Moor. In other huts there were machineguns watched over by grisly old sergeants. The offices were set apart and labelled 'No Admit-tance' and 'Keep Out'. Here and there guards were mounted on sentry-go. Why, there was even a stretch of barbed-wire about the place and over the sand dunes! The very sight of the huts depressed me – if only we had been under canvas! It was like a nightmare to be back in such surroundings, the nightmare I dreaded most: recapture.

And the reports which other pilots gave me were not encouraging. The place was full to overflowing, there had not been many demands from squadrons recently, there was a shortage of practice machines, and a waiting-list a mile long. Many of the pilots did not care; they had been out to France several times before and were content to wait their turn. Some of them had been waiting two or three weeks, and were expecting to stay for as many more . . . 'They also serve who only stand and wait' . . . Was *Milton* ever in the Pilots' Pool? It was certainly my own idea of a Paradise for the Lost. I was bored and discouraged.

During my first day more than twenty pilots arrived; not half a dozen left. There was nothing to do all day and nothing but a bar to sit in at night. On the second day the same thing happened: many officers coming in, few going out. Someone who had been to the office told me that the list of pilots was in a terrible muddle; the single-seater people were mixed up with the heavy bombers, and it might be weeks before things were straightened out. The only fellow I knew at all well departed for a squadron, but he went alone. I began to feel as desperate as at Zomdorf, this business of getting back was worse than I had thought. There was no flying, and on the coast we could not hear the guns. The wind hummed, but in wires that were barbed not streamlined.

Early on the morning of the third day I went to the office to have a look around. There were many pilots hanging about, some old, some new; they were giving particulars about themselves to be entered on the new lists which were being compiled by a couple of clerks. Some of us strolled into the orderly-room – the CO being absent at breakfast – to look at the lists, at the numbers of those squadrons requiring pilots, the photographs of enemy machines, and so on. I was reading through some routine orders when all at once I caught sight of the new list of single-seater pilots. It was lying beside the typewriter upon which it had just been made out by one of the clerks, ready for submitting to the CO as soon as he came in.

I glanced down it. It was very long, covering two pages of foolscap gummed together. Pilots' names were thick on the paper as autumn leaves on Vallombrosa. It took me a long time to reach my own – near the foot of the page! Just as I found it one of the clerks came by.

'I say, Corporal, surely my name ought to be higher than that,' I exclaimed, bitter with disappointment. 'I've been here three days already. I can't wait for ever!' He laughed as he came up to me. He was a friendly sort of fellow.

'Some of them have been here for three weeks, sir. But perhaps there's been a mistake. Let me see – which is your name?' I reached forward to point it out. As I did so my sleeve caught against some light object upon the table.

'Look out!' cried the Corporal.

But he was just too late. A river of ink streamed over the page and cascaded to the floor. The bottle rolled slowly through the black stream, splashing over the names.

'O-o-oh ...' said the Corporal. 'You —' He paused, only the regulation respect for rank preventing a comment upon my parentage. 'You — you've spilt the ink!'

'I'm frightfully sorry,' I told him. 'I couldn't help it. Bottle on the table –
uncorked – caught in my sleeve – an accident. I can't tell you how sorry
I am.'

He was kind enough to be pacified at once.

'That's all right, sir; it can't be helped. Trouble is it's the only completed list we've got. And the CO will want to see it – he'll be here in a
minute.'

I bustled about as anxious as he.

'Then let's get it re-typed at once. Come on! I'll help you. Sit down.
Got some foolscap? Right. I'll read the list out – I can manage to see
through the ink. Ready? First, the heading …'

'Oh, I know the heading, sir,' he answered, settling down before the
typewriter. 'It reads: "List of Pilots"'. He began to tap the keys.
'… "Pilots for Single-seat Fighters" …' *Tap-tap-tap. Tap-a-tap. Tap.*
'SE 5, Sopwith Camels and Dolphins.' *Tap-tap-tap.* "Name and Rank."
Tap-tap-a-tap. 'Now, sir, if you please?'

'Yes, what is it?'

'The first name, please, sir.'

'The first name?'

'Yes, sir, the first.'

'Lieutenant D. Grinnell-Milne.'

Tap-tap. Tap-a-tap. Tap-tap …

After an early lunch a Crossley tender bore me off in the direction of the
front. I was sorry for those who had been waiting for three weeks, but then
I had been waiting for three years.

*   *   *

Those drivers of Crossley tenders who ferried air-pilots across Northern
France always seemed to me a most mysterious lot of men. Their knowledge of the country, of the roads and byroads – some of which I was never
able to find again – smacked of the supernatural. The way in which they
drove, unerringly and in silence, direct to squadrons of whose location,
of whose very numbers the passengers were ignorant, attained to the
miraculous. They were a race of men apart, inscrutable, possessed of a
knowledge beyond our divination; of a breed descended perhaps from
some brief union between Charon and Nemesis, for while they carried us
behind them they were the arbiters of our destiny. There was an uncanny
family likeness about all of them, particularly in the set of the jaw.

A curious similarity, too, linked my first journey to this my second.
True, the first commencing at St. Omer had ended, after a halt at Aire,
upon the banks of the Lys, whereas the second took me from Berck to

south of Doullens. (And there is a world of difference between Flanders and Picardy.) But there were other close resemblances, close enough to bring back vivid memories of what seemed a long-forgotten war in a by-gone century. It was, in fact, within a month of three years since I had last approached the front in a Crossley tender. The season, the weather, were almost the same. The roads, winding over undulating fields or rushing straight down long tree-lined avenues, were white and dusty. Lorries were more plentiful, and ambulances and staff-cars, but horse transport was still in evidence. There were still farm carts on the roads, and carts laden with hay. There were still peasants in blue smocks, and wooden shoes, in the fields, cattle in the farmyards, women at the doors, and smoke from old chimneys. France in the back areas had not, I fancied, changed much in a hundred years – although no doubt Corot would have been surprised to find his dancing nymphs replaced among the poplars in the meadows by sinister Portuguese troops and Chinese coolies.

But the lack of change behind the lines made me wonder again whether I had not imagined the period of captivity. It was hard to realise that I had been absent during the immensity of those years between. So many men – millions of them! – had marched down these same roads since I had passed there. Day and night for a thousand days the guns had muttered behind the horizon to the east, rising to thunder during those incredible battles – the Somme, Arras, Messines, Ypres, Cambrai and the great German attack. Had I really missed so much? I could scarcely believe it, could scarcely believe that battalions, divisions, armies of men had vanished, that a score of young men whom I had known intimately – at school, in the infantry, in the Flying Corps – had no longer a voice in that everlasting clamour of war a few miles away. I was not 'coming back'; it was into another war that I was being drawn, as though I myself had been killed during the Long Reconnaissance on that blustering December day in 1915, to be reincarnated, after an uneasy stretch in purgatory, amid surroundings familiar enough but amongst men unknown to me. Not one of the half-dozen pilots in the tender knew any one I knew, and they spoke of squadrons and their histories with an ease that left me silent and alone with my memories.

They left the tender, those six pilots, at various points along the road where squadrons had their headquarters, until at length I was the only one remaining behind the taciturn driver. That, too, was just as three years before I found myself wondering to what sort of a temporary home I was being driven. Would I meet with the same chilling reception as in the barge? Would I find a Starched Shirt in command, a Growl to insist upon salutes and standings to attention, a Foxy to make me feel 'all goosey'? I was very much afraid that my history might repeat itself far too accurately.

We came to a farm, turned off the main road, bumped over the ruts of a winding track. My head began to nod, for the drive had been long and the evening was warm. When, after one exceptionally long doze, I opened my eyes, I saw a line of poplars and thought myself back upon the Lys ... But there was no river here; a wide expanse of open field was spread before the poplars, themselves bordering a wood upon the brow of a low hill. There were sheds at the side of the field, two groups of them with the usual adjuncts of transport lorries, workshops, store tents. We passed the first group – I had already began to collect my belongings, but the driver shook his head – and driving round the aerodrome went slowly down a lane between the second group of sheds and the small, dense wood. At a gate leading into an orchard we came to a halt.

'Here you are, sir,' the driver announced, speaking to me for the first time while, with a stub of pencil, he ticked my name off the list. 'This is your squadron. Name of the place? Valheureux.'

I got down. The driver hailed a couple of men near one of the sheds to help him unload my kit, and I turned away to advance reluctantly through the gate into the orchard, wishing I had one of my prison friends with me. Now that I had arrived I positively dreaded the first moments in a strange Mess with strange pilots. My feet lagged in spite of the necessity to go forward – under the eyes of the tender-driver I could not turn back – and I had time to look about me. Scattered among the fruit-trees were the officers' quarters, bell-tents and small huts, the grass growing long between them. Ahead of me, half-hidden by other trees, was a large Mess-tent connected by a short canvas passageway with a wooden building rather like a cricket pavilion. It was painted green and had small lattice windows, a low sloping roof and a wooden porch along the front. Evidently the Mess. A comfortable looking place, snug and homelike tucked away amid the trees and lush grass. I hoped devoutly that the inmates would not turn out to be unbearable ...

A voice called to me from the porch; a young pilot, whom I recognised as one I had known in England, rose from a camp-chair and hurried towards me as I looked hesitatingly around.

'By Jove! I'm awfully glad to see you – what luck your coming here! I didn't think you would get out to France for months yet. How did you do it? Come on into the Mess. I'll show you round the Squadron presently ...'

As a first step I could not have wished for better. To be greeted as an old friend by someone, to be told that he was 'awfully glad' to see me was just the tonic I needed. Confidence began to return with the first sip.

On the porch I met and shook hands with two pilots, both friendly and both Americans: Larry B— and Johnnie S—, and then my friend led me into the main room of the 'Pavilion'. It was empty just then, so that I was able to get my bearings before meeting the rest of the Squadron.

'I say, do you realise what Squadron this is?' my friend went on – the corruption of his name most generally used in the Squadron was 'Shutters.' 'You're in luck to be sent here. This is the most famous Squadron in France – Ball was in it, and McCudden, and Rhys Davies, and a flock of other…'

I thought of a dark, stone-vaulted room in Zorrndorf and of a Scots pilot, recently captured, telling me of the squadrons and the airmen in France: 'the best o' the bunch – Captain Ball …' That pilot had been taken at the close of the winter's fighting on the Somme. He was not a single-seater pilot himself, but he had known all about Ball. And what he then told me had set my ears ringing once again with the fancied roaring of aero-engines and the music of the wires … Now, of a sudden, it seemed that no time at all had passed since I had heard him speak. Zorndorf – aeroplanes on the Somme and over Cambrai – the concentrated efforts to escape – the frontier – freedom! – and so to France, to Ball's Squadron: it was the only logical sequence. Once more the army was attacking, past the ruins of the Somme, on towards Cambrai and St Quentin, and the Hindenburg Line. The enemy had been held, repulsed, was at length being forced back. I was ready to play my own small part in the air again. But Captain Ball was dead…

Shutters went on speaking.

'And, do you know, the Squadron has brought down more German machines than any other in France! Look at that list of Honours!'

He pointed to the far wall. Beneath a wooden propeller of German make and between two black canvas crosses cut from enemy aircraft, a three-ply board was fixed in a carved wooden frame. The number of the Squadron was at the head: below were the names of men who had won decorations.

Bravery, I suppose, is relative like everything else, and the displaying of it in such a manner as to earn a decoration must generally be a matter of chance, yet in this squadron the number of the awards and the period over which they were spread under successive commanders seemed to prove beyond doubt that the work of its pilots had been consistently courageous. Ball headed the list. The date against his name was 6th June 1917.

From that date until my arrival a year and three months had passed, and in that time the members of the Squadron had collected two VCs, six DSOs, fourteen MCs, eight bars to MCs, and six DFCs.

I remember laughing out loud as I looked at that long list – much to Shutters surprise.

'What's the matter?' he demanded, rather crossly. 'Aren't there enough names there?'

'Oh, yes – almost too many. I was thinking of the Squadron I belonged to in 1915. There we had one MC between the whole lot of us. It would have been funny to have seen that lonely name on a board in the barge!'

'Perhaps you didn't have the same opportunities in those days,' Shutters was kind enough to remark. 'Who was your CO?'

'The Starched Shirt,' I told him, giving the name.

'Never heard of him,' murmured Shutters. And somehow I found his answer full of meaning: the Starched Shirt was a General now, in charge of training or something, a successful senior officer, not a bad fellow at heart, and fond of Surtees, heard of him. His name would not be remembered when the far-off days of peace brought airmen together to talk over old exploits, his name would never figure upon the honours roll of any squadron. But these men – these names headed by that of 'Captain Ball, VC, DSO, MC, Lègion d'honneur' – they would not soon be forgotten by those who fought. Indeed the final and greatest Decoration to which so many had already attained would ensure that their names lived on forevermore. So that on joining such a Squadron and seeing such a list for the first time, one might well believe oneself to be standing at a parting of the ways; the way of the excellent Starched Shirts of this world, or the way of Ball, Rhy Davies, McCudden and others.

How did Gilbert put it?

'Is life a boon?
If so, it must befall
That Death, whene'er he call,
Must call too soon!'

Too soon? I forgot about the squadron on the banks of the Lys – and read slowly through the names on my new Squadron's roll of honour . . .

'Let's go down to the sheds,' said Shutters impatiently.

*   *   *

On the way back from the aerodrome I met the CO for the first time. I was following Shutters along a narrow path through the orchard and the wood which surrounded it, when he came out from a trim wooden hut amid the trees. Shutters stopped and saluted. I did likewise.

'Hallo – what's the game?' said the Major. He was tall, lean, young; his small moustache seemed almost black by contrast with his exceedingly pale face. He wore the uniform of the 9th Lancers, Wings, and a Military Cross ribbon.

'New pilot, sir, just arrived,' Shutters announced. And then like an ass he added, after mentioning my name: 'He's an escaped prisoner.'

The Major smiled; but I could see that he was scared. He evidently remembered something about the authorities' attitude to prisoners. He asked questions in a mild manner, but quickly and to the point. Where had I served before, when had I been captured, when escaped?

'Good Lord ... I suppose it's all right?' he exclaimed at the end.

'Oh, perfectly all right, sir,' I answered airily. 'I've fixed it all up with the Air Ministry.'

He was silent, and for a moment I was horrified by the thought that he was going to announce his intention of making inquiries. Memories of the King's voice came back to me:

'What are you going to do now?' – Going to France – 'Will they let you?' It would be awful to be sent back now after having got so far – like being recaptured on the frontier!

The Major regarded me steadily while his smile slowly broadened. He did not speak, but I seemed to read the word 'Liar!' in his eyes. And I smiled back at him, for I felt sure it was a friendly reproach.

'Well, I suppose you're anxious to get some of your own from enemy aircraft, back on the Huns,' he said at length. 'I expect you've got a score or two to pay off.'

I told him that that was my main idea in returning and that I should like to start as soon as possible.

'Oh, there's plenty of time,' he replied. 'It's a rule that new pilots don't go over the lines until they've been three weeks with the Squadron.

Three weeks! I protested. In three weeks anything might happen. I wanted to get going at once. I had been over the lines before – that must be obvious or I would not have been captured – I had plenty of flying-hours to my credit, experience with SE 5s and so on. The Major went on smiling.

'I dare say I might make an exception in your case,' he conceded as he turned away towards the sheds. 'You'll have to do some formation and firing practice first, though. You don't want to be shot down the first time you go on patrol over the lines!'

Those last words came back to me afterwards.

*   *   *

It was getting late. Shutters and I strolled back to the Mess, where already most of the pilots had gathered for cocktails. The majority were very young – that is, few of them were any older than myself, and few wore decorations, for the Squadron had had heavy losses in the past month or two. I will not claim that I was welcomed like a long lost friend, because I did not know any of them by sight or by name, but there was a hint of geniality about their greeting that put me at ease. At first I was more diffident than they were, since, with memories of my first night in the barge, I rather expected to be given the cold shoulder, but with the arrival of the second round of drinks, what little ice there was melted rapidly.

Everyone was in good spirits. Two German machines had been shot down that morning. The Squadron's total bag since coming to France was nearing the 400-mark – an average of almost one a day over a period of more than a year! Of course, things were slowing up because the older German aircraft over which the SE 5s of the Squadron had had an un-doubted superiority were being replaced by more efficient machines. The Fokker biplane was the principal enemy to be fought now, and against that good little machine the SE had to be careful. 'Dive and zoom!' I was told, 'dive and zoom – don't try a dog-fight with them until you've had plenty of experience. They can generally outmanoeuvre you.'

'But we're faster on the level and in a dive,' said the American Larry B—. 'Keep the old SE going fast and you can beat anything in the sky.'

'Yes, but those darned Fokkers can outclimb us,' put in a Canadian Flight Commander. 'The best thing to do is to get height at the beginning of the patrol, manoeuvre for the sun – then, when you see your Huns, half-roll and dive on to their tails.'

'And keep going,' Larry B— repeated. 'Don't stop to argue unless you're mighty sure of yourself – just dive straight through them and zoom up later to see what's left. Then you can half-roll and dive again ...'

I was back in France. In a famous and efficient fighting squadron whose pilots were still eager and ready to add to their laurels. Their feelings, their desires, their ideals were also mine. There was no cold water to quench enthusiasm here. To some of the youngest pilots naturally I was something of a curiosity. A sort of Rip Van Winkle of the air, who com-pared all that they told of modern fighting with conditions existing in 1915; but they soon realised I was keener on flying than on talking about the past, which was all that really mattered to them. And to me their old-new jargon spoken within sound of the guns was very thrilling.

Presently 'Gilly' came into the Mess. 'Gilly' was the name of the CO, though not generally used to his face. I had not noticed any particular stiffness about him at the first meeting, but now, the day's work over, he seemed to have unbent completely.

'Well, chaps, how about it? A slight celebration tonight I think, what?' were his first exclamations. 'Now, then, where's the Newt?' The 'Newt,' I discovered later, was the diminutive adjutant. 'Newt, go and tell the band to fall in here at once. And – where's that Mess-corporal? – Corporal, ask all the officers what they want to drink ...'

A band? I was amazed as I watched the six members of the orchestra file in by a side door past the small bar and pantry. A piano stood in a corner of the room; drums, violins, a double-bass gathered round it – men of the Squadron led by a broad-shouldered, moustachioed Sergeant.

'Strike up!' ordered Gilly; 'and start off with the Squadron Tune.'

To some it might make pleasant reading were I able to record that, with the Squadron Commander and his gallant officers standing stiffly to attention, the orchestra played a selection from 'Pomp and Circumstance,' beginning with a noble and full-throated chorus of 'Land of Hope and Glory.' Or perhaps, in view of the large proportion of Americans present, 'The Star-Spangled Banner' would have been appropriate, and I am sure it would have been more decorous had we intoned the Hymn to the Royal Air Force – 'who ride upon the viewless air' – or some equally grim anthem ... The melody chosen by the Squadron to which I now had the honour to belong could only, I am afraid, be regarded as frivolous. It was called 'The Darktown Strutters' Ball', and the first line of its refrain informed some unnamed lady that: 'I'll be there to get you in a taxi, honey.' But nobody objected to the words, and the rhythm was invigorating. It was a damn' good tune! And the orchestra played wonderfully well, superbly, I thought. We shouted the chorus over the third and fourth round of drinks. And it may have been the cocktails, but I began to bless the good fortune which had brought me to this Squadron.

After dinner Gilly, becoming solemn for a moment, read out the names of those going on the Dawn Patrol. I was foolishly disappointed to find that my own name was not amongst them.

*   *   *

On the way to my tent that night I made a detour through the orchard so as to come out into the open on the eastern side of the aerodrome. I was impelled by some strange excitement – not alcoholic! – to see what was happening in the direction of the front lines. It was a dark night, but the horizon was aglow with intermittent gun flashes. We were too far from the retiring line of battle for me to see the flares sent up from the trenches, but their wavering light shone from behind the skyline with unearthly effect, as if playful giants were striking box after box of titanic matches. Owing to the recent German retirements the distance to the front was a good 15 miles, so that the sounds which reached me were softened and confused. A continual vague rumour kept the night alive, occasionally a long burst of machine-gun fire would rise and fall as though borne upon an impalpable breeze, but in the main it was the thudding of the guns which alone was plainly audible, the flashes which gave the scene reality.

Waste of time to seek for analogies and metaphors: the sounds of war are not like the sea beating furiously upon a rocky coast, not altogether like the raging of an immense and savage beast, nor yet like the subdued murmur of violent strife in some modern Vanity Fair. And there can be no comparison between the thunder of the skies and an artillery bombardment, since fair weather follows the storm, which is not always the case after war. But, apart from all else, apart from the horrors and the barbarism, gun-fire when heard from a reasonable distance is more inspiriting. It reminds one of the urgency of the job on hand, of the necessity to see it through; it seems to call with an imperious voice demanding fresh effort and sacrifice in an everlasting struggle. It would be well if we could hear it in peacetime. Not so near as to be wrecking our homes and driving us away from our work into dug-outs, but just beyond the skyline, a menacing reminder of the reality from which we hide our faces and seek so pitifully to escape. Because of senseless devastation, gun-fire has an evil ring; but it is at least sharp, decisive, unmistakable, far-reaching, whereas the clamour of tongues in eternal conference now replacing the cannonade is often vain, discouraging, and without echo in the hearts of men. Gun-fire has been known to bring nations to their senses, it has decided swiftly and not always wrongly problems which years of parleying have failed to solve, for there may sometimes be virtue in the sword, as in the surgeon's knife. It was not military violence alone which prompted Alexander to cut the Gordian knot; that gesture has its significance in the world today ...

Just then, I admit it freely, gun-fire held the utmost significance for me. The last time that sound had come to me from the front in France, I had stood peering *westwards* from the window of a prison camp in Germany. Now I faced over open ground – to the *east*!

From between the orchard trees at my back came the strains of the orchestra playing the final piece of the evening: the Squadron's tune, 'Tomorrow night at the Darktown Strutters' Ball.' Tomorrow – I would fly again in France. Only a practice flight, but with what meaning for me! The Squadron lay not far from the Somme battlefields. I would fly to the south of Bapaume, fly over the very place where I had landed to become a prisoner.

*   *   *

It was actually something like ten days before I was allowed to cross the lines officially. I say 'officially' because of course I could not resist the temptation to sneak across during various practice flights; but not too far over, for I was mortally afraid of displeasing my new Squadron-commander and perhaps being sent home 'in disgrace', as Foxy would have called it, before I had had time to achieve anything. Gilly was willing to let me take my full share of the Squadron's work as soon as possible, but he was right in holding me back. It would have been very awkward, when some of the Air Ministry officials concerned were not even aware of my presence in France, had I disappeared or been recaptured on my first flight.

Every day I was allowed to take up an SE, either for formation flying or for firing practice at a ground target, so that gradually I became more confident of doing my share alongside those pilots whose experience seemed, at first, so much greater than any I could hope to acquire. Firing at a ground target was good practice for attacks on trenches and troops as well as for aerial combats, and with hints and tips from Gilly himself I began to learn something of both forms of fighting. The Squadron was frequently employed on operations such as aerodrome raids, bombing of troops and transport, and harassing tactics generally, in addition to its normal occupation of high altitude fighting, for the ebb and flow which, since the German offensive in March, had come into the hitherto stagnant position – war had greatly increased the importance of guerilla attacks by fast single-seaters. 'Risky work,' I was told, 'but lots of fun.' Later on indeed these operations became of such value as to outweigh by far the bringing down of a few more enemy aeroplanes.

Meanwhile it was our business to be ready for both jobs and I took to the firing practice seriously, believing that, as Gilly had said, there would be plenty of time to pay off old scores. I had waited for so long, a little more patience was easy to command. The war would slow down during the winter months whilst I gained experience; in the spring and early summer I would be ready to put forth my maximum effort for the final victories. Casualties, however, brought suddenly near the day when I was to be sent off to measure my skill and my luck. A Flight Commander was wounded a couple of days after my arrival; then a young pilot was reported missing, another killed, a third crashed, a fourth fell ill and was taken to hospital. Not very heavy losses, but persistent enough to make replacement necessary even by such novices as myself. An aerodrome raid – at which I was a mere spectator, high up in the sky with the protective flight – was hailed as a success, but it cost the life of the young American, Larry B—. And then another pilot was reported missing ...

And thus stepping into dead men's shoes – or more accurately into the cockpit of a vanished pilot – I found my name one evening at the tail end of the list for the Dawn Patrol.

*   *   *

The curious fate which seemed to steer my course throughout the war now showed itself clearly. For with that very first Dawn Patrol my patience went by the boards, my carefully laid plans were blown to pieces as though they had been struck by a direct hit from an Archie shell, and I became involved in a veritable whirlwind of events, fights, raids, and accidents which did not cease blowing until the war itself ended. Almost literally a whirlwind, for the machines I flew were also caught up by it, battered, shot down, damaged beyond repair.

And yet the day began in a normal manner. We left the aerodrome in the grey light, flying east into the brilliant sky of a perfect morning, climbing steadily to cross the lines south-west of Cambrai and head for the rising sun, testing our guns as we went. Below us lay the ruined country of which not even Sir Thomas Browne could have said that it had survived the drums and tramplings of three conquests. On both sides the artillery was busy, presaging a heavy day in the air. Presently Archie opened up on us, keeping his usual fairly safe distance so that I rejoiced to hear the old familiar sound of his chronic cough. At 18,000 feet we turned north-east, and a few moments later, somewhere above the line Valenciennes Cambrai, we sighted a large enemy formation.

I say 'we' because I suppose everyone saw the enemy machine at more or less the same time, but actually it didn't much matter whether I sighted them or not. I was the last man on the right of the top, protective flight; it was for the leader of the lower flight to find and attack the enemy – which is what he did. Hardly had I recognised the distinctive silhouette of Fokker biplanes than I saw a red light shoot up from our leader and down we went in a steep dive to the attack. For a moment it seemed as if the enemy were going to dive too, then his formation broke up, scattered and engaged our machines. This caused our own flights also to break up, each man going after the enemy nearest to him, and in a few seconds, instead of neat Vs manoeuvring for position, the air was full of machines hurtling in all directions like traffic at a badly regulated street intersection. The, for me, ticklish operation of a dog-fight was in full swing.

'Dive and zoom,' they had told me, so I dived and zoomed. For an instant a Fokker flashed full into my sights; I dived hard, pressed the trigger-release and prayed for victory. But with what seemed no more than a flick of the pilot's wrist he swerved off at right-angles, and a second later shots from another enemy crackled past my head. 'Dive and zoom!' I made haste to obey. 'If the enemy fire is too hot – hard rudder and no bank – sideslip!' I tried that too ...

All at once I found myself outside the dog-fight. I looked round hastily. Two of the enemy had gone down as the result of our first attack, but already the fight was practically over, with the enemy chasing our people away. 'Attack – dive and zoom ...' it had been, now it was 'dive for home'. Until we could get clear and reform the V, it was each man for himself. Fortunately my last zoom had taken me above and away from the main group of the enemy, for I was alone; having started at the tail-end of the flight, I had been left a considerable distance behind. Opening my engine to full throttle, I pushed the nose down along the shortest course for our own lines.

And then, looking about to see that no enemy was sneaking up to get a shot in from my tail, I noticed something very odd. The clear blue sky was streaked and criss-crossed with the smoke of tracer bullets, the thin lines of greyish vapour shining in the bright sunlight. Archie puffs were dotted here and there, and a dark trail showed where a machine had gone down in flames. But there was something else. A thick blue-grey streamer of smoke was festooned over the scene of the recent fight – circling, diving, zooming – following the course of one of the machines engaged. I could see no craft, friendly or hostile, from which this streamer could be coming, but glancing over my shoulder I saw that it became thicker and darker the nearer it came to me ... I jerked my head round anxiously. It came from my own machine!

But I was not on fire, that was my first joyful thought. The thick oily smoke came from the starboard exhaust pipe, and watching the end of the pipe I saw pieces of metal come trickling out. Something was very much the matter. One of those infernal Fokker bullets must have hit the engine – yes, that's what it was! I had heard the click and rattle of a couple of shots getting home on the machine at the beginning of the fight, and now that I came to notice it, the engine was vibrating a lot, the revolution-counter wavering slowly downwards. Already the figures were getting low – 1,700 feet, 1,650 feet, 1,600 feet. I must hurry up and recross the lines! Luckily the enemy were now a good way behind; firing spasmodically but harmlessly. I looked over the side to make sure that I was following the best course.

We had gone a long distance east to find the enemy and the usual west wind had carried us still farther during the fight. I had made good headway so far, but as near as I could judge the lines were 12 to 15 miles away. Cambrai lay beyond my starboard wing tip, below were open fields – a queerly reminiscent stretch of country ... I glanced back. Valenciennes showed up unpleasantly close, almost directly under my tailplane. And even as I looked, the engine shuddered, dropped another hundred revolutions. The altimeter pointed to less than 14,000 feet. Some 15 miles to go, against the wind, with a failing engine ... Good heavens! I had done all this before. Exactly the same thing over this identical course. Valenciennes, the west wind, engine trouble – it was happening all over again. I was about to be recaptured and there was nothing I could do to prevent it. A bit of history, unimportant to any one save myself, was bent on repeating itself. I was furiously angry and desperately unhappy by turns ... 8,000 feet from the ground – only! – then 7,000 feet, 6,500 feet. The engine was running much worse, it was going to seize up altogether presently, and the lines were still many miles off. The last of the enemy machines had disappeared, but so had the last of my own people; lucky beggars, they must be safe already. And I was going to land – crash, in all probability – in the enemy trenches west of Cambrai.

Archie crept close and a cloud passed over the sun. It was so bumpy at low altitudes that I lost height more rapidly. There was heavy fighting going on below, clouds of gas and smoke, and a terrific bombardment. I could hear it plainly above the tired rumble of the engine and the dreary humming of the wires. I was getting close – but I was hearing the guns from the wrong side once again. If only the wind would drop ...

At 3,000 feet the engine gave an unearthly groan and subsided altogether. I switched off. The bombardment became deafeningly loud.

* * *

I must suppose that Fate wished to show me both sides of the picture – what might have happened with a bit of luck nearly three years before. Because I landed amid the shell holes near the village of Quéant, about 1½ miles behind the British front lines. Somehow or other the machine had managed to drift over the trenches in spite of Archie and I landed her, much to my surprise, without breaking anything. But I was still very worried when I got out of the cockpit; the sensation of being doomed to recapture had been so strong I could not easily shake it off. Anxiously I looked into the cubby-hole behind the pilot's seat to see if the flare for setting her alight were safely stowed. The guns were loud, but even now they seemed to be firing in the wrong direction. I had lost my bearings a little in the last moments of that uncomfortable glide ...

A voice hailed me. I jumped round in alarm. But it was a friendly head which poked itself out of a dugout doorway.

'Come on in,' said the owner of the head. 'Must have been cold up there this morning. Have some whisky!'

I did.

And later I got on the phone to the Squadron, spoke to the Newt.

'I'll send a tender for you,' he said. 'Glad you're safe, we thought you were missing. Don't forget to bring back the watch!'

The eight-day luminous watch was the one item on the instrument board which appealed to all men. It was easily detachable, so easily that any machine left untended for more than a few minutes was invariably looted of its valuable time-piece. The first thing a pilot had to remember, no matter how serious the crash, was to unscrew the watch. But the morning's events must have unsettled me for I left the wretched thing in the machine.

The tender arrived at noon and that same evening I dined again in the Mess instead of, as I had for a while feared, in St Quentin goal. The Newt was a little upset at my having forgotten the watch, but Gilly was good enough to say that he was pleased to see me back; he too, it seemed, had had a nasty feeling that I might have been retaken, and I think he knew what the thought of recapture meant to me. That, however, was something more than one of the junior pilots understood. At dinner I happened to sit next to him. He came from somewhere near Glasgow and so was called, I suppose inevitably Jock.

'What was the Major talking about?' he asked. 'Something about your having been a prisoner – surely you were never such a fool as to get captured?'

I admitted that it was so, that I had been just such a fool.

'But, good God, man – how did you manage it? And you were there *two and a half years*? Unwounded at that? I can't believe it!'

'I'm afraid it's true,' I told him sadly. 'And it really couldn't be helped.'

'Nonsense! No one ever needs to be taken prisoner.'

'Supposing it happens to you some day, what then?'

'I'll get back before I'm caught.'

I began to feel uncomfortable – worried for him.

'But if your engine fails when you're, say, 15 or 20 miles on the wrong side of the lines?'

'I'll glide home.'

'And if the wind is against you and you haven't enough height to glide over the front?'

'Those are absurd suppositions, but if it did happen that I was forced to land in enemy territory I would know what to do.'

'What's that?'

'Run away – hide in a wood – take cover somewhere. And crawl back after dark through the trenches. I'd know how to do it – I've served in the Infantry.' Poor fellow! So might I have spoken in the days of the barge on the Lys.

'Well, if you didn't have the luck to do any of those things, you might still be taken prisoner?'

'And be put in a German goal? Pouf – I'd be out of that before they'd had time to lock the doors! But I'd never surrender – not unwounded like you did.'

I rose in wrath at that, called heaven to witness that he was boasting, cursed him for an impudent fool, and – though God knows I am no prophet – foretold his capture within a fortnight ... Afterwards I felt rather foolish at having become so heated, there was no sense in feeling aggrieved at such happy ignorance. And as for my prophecy of capture, it was unfortunately far more likely that Jock would be killed, wounded, or injured in a crash than taken prisoner within that specified time of two weeks. I did not really wish him any ill-luck.

Ten days later the Dawn Patrol returned after a sharp engagement with a large number of Fokkers. It was my morning off and I stood on the aerodrome counting the SEs as they came in to land. Two were missing. One of them contained Jock.

My sorrow was genuine, for the loss was the Squadron's and I had forgotten my silly prophecy; besides it seemed probable by all accounts that Jock had been killed. But before the end of the week we heard that he was safe – a prisoner and unwounded. Then, I must confess, I laughed. And I think we all wondered if we should not soon see him back, a free man after breaking gaol and crawling through the lines. Presently we forgot all about him – as they must have forgotten about me on the Lys.

After the war someone met him in London. He was just back from Germany, talking very little and feeling rather *piano*. He had been returned with the canaries and the knitting ... As I remember, this is the only time when a prophecy of mine has come true; but it is not the only occasion on which I have been reproached for having surrendered.

* * *

At some time during the war Mr Rudyard Kipling wrote a number of verses dedicated to various categories of people engaged in the struggle. In a moment of poetic aberration he wrote of a young pilot diving through clouds, 'his milk-teeth yet unshed' ... Merciful heavens! we were young, but not that childish. Are not first teeth generally dropped by the time a boy reached the age of twelve, fourteen at the latest? There cannot have been a fighting pilot in France under seventeen, the majority were certainly over twenty years of age, and by St Apollina, patron saint of dentists, there were no loose teeth in Gilly's Squadron. Think of stopping in the middle of a dog-fight to spit out a couple of pre-molars!

However, even supposing Mr Kipling's picture to have been accurately painted, I would assuredly have lost the whole galaxy on the afternoon of 28 September. I came near to losing more than that.

'Now then, chaps, a big show today,' Gilly had told us in the morning. 'There's a full-size war in progress – attack on the Hindenburg Line. We do high patrols first, and this afternoon trench-strafing. The Boche is taking it in the neck – got to stop his reinforcements coming up and harass his retreat, if any. Now off you go – dive and zoom – and if their fire gets too heavy remember the safest thing is to *keep low down!*'

We left at intervals in flights of three, loaded up with ammunition and four 25-pound bombs apiece. My own party, led by a senior pilot, made for Cambrai, crossed the lines at 2,000 feet and began circling the country to the south of the town looking for targets. There was a terrific battle going on underneath, to the west of the Scheldt Canal; the air was bumpy with explosions and with the flight of high trajectory shells. Comparatively undamaged country was rapidly being battered to pieces, villages were collapsing like sand castles overwhelmed by the tide, churches went down in clouds of dust, farms and isolated houses blazed furiously. Of course, the main clamour of warfare was inaudible to us above the roaring of our engines and the persistent singing of the wires, so that flying low it was ever surprising to see, without warning sound, a mass of broken earth fly into the air as a heavy shell burst nearby, or to observe a stout wall suddenly collapse in smoke and débris without so much as a murmur having reached one's ears. Rather like a silent film ... Few troops were to be seen on the German side and little movement. At first it was hard to find suitable targets, especially since we were flying in formation.

Keeping formation even at high altitudes always bothered me when a scrap was imminent, I suppose because my early training had formed an instinctive desire to be alone and unhampered. Certainly I never learnt to feel comfortable fighting in V-formation and near the ground the proximity of other pilots was to me intolerable. On this occasion our first few dives at small parties of enemy infantry seemed positively feeble, for we were worrying far too much about keeping the right distance from one another, and about pulling out of each dive as soon as the leader did, to aim properly or to fire with any enthusiasm. Moreover, cruising about at some 1,500 feet from the ground we were offering an easy target for machine-gunners as well as for Archie. At the first objective worthy of my bombs I decided to break away from the others and work on my own.

Presently my interest was aroused by a small railway station south-east of Cambrai. It seemed at first glance to be deserted, but we had come gradually lower and I happened to notice some half-a-dozen German soldiers standing motionless beside what must have been the waiting-room. In their field-grey uniforms they were practically invisible and I should never have seen them but for the white circles of their upturned faces. It was funny seeing German faces so close to me again. Like being half-way back in prison. Funny? Well, I didn't exactly hate them, but I disliked them a good deal and this was war; I broke off from the formation, circled round and dropped two bombs.

Since I was not more than 100 feet up the bombs made a nasty sort of *Clang–Clang*! under my SE's tail, but there was no other response from the ground. When I looked back the signal-box was hidden by a cloud of black smoke and there was a big dent in the roof of the waiting-room ... So far so good! I searched around for other targets. This was rather fun, I thought, and not too dangerous if one kept as low down as Gilly advised. It is next to impossible to hit a machine dodging round trees and house-tops at 120-or-more miles an hour, but the trouble was that to put in a reasonably long burst of fire one had to zoom up to about 500 feet where concentrated rifle and machinegun fire was apt to become much too hot. However, with a bit of turning, twisting, and sideslipping I hoped to counter that.

By this time the other two machines of the flight had vanished, had found other targets I supposed. I was alone again; if I got shot down no one would know where I had gone to. Time enough to think of that later ... I found some Germans in trenches – half-rolled, dived and zoomed. Then a party strolling through a cutting between two hills – dived and zoomed again. I heard them return my fire, but they did no damage, and a few moments later I saw a cart drawn by two horses moving briskly down a road. There were a number of men in the cart, with machine guns – I saw the details clearly as I passed within 100 feet of them. I don't know what they were doing, whether retiring or going up the front, for the winding road ran approximately parallel to the firing line. But it was a tempting target, and again the sight of those German uniforms gave me an odd sensation of annoyance. I dived from 800 feet.

When he heard me coming the man on the box whipped up his horses. Why he did that I cannot say, for there was nowhere for him to go, and it made little difference to me whether his cart travelled at 8 or 16 miles an hour. I suppose the men in the cart got excited when my first shots fell amongst them, perhaps they yelled. At all events the horses bolted, left the road, the cart tipped over and rolled down a grass bank into a stream. My last glimpse of the men who had been on the box showed me a face strangely reminiscent, at that distance and in that second, of an extremely disagreeable *Feldwebel* at Fort Zomdorf. I felt that I had paid off a score... And when I pulled out of the dive the wires were screaming triumphantly like the blare of brass instruments in the ride of the Valkyries.

I stared ahead. Beyond a line of trees three or four flashes of yellow light winked at me. Guns! I was over an artillery emplacement. Not very well concealed, they had evidently moved up hurriedly. I had two bombs left – just the thing! Approaching from behind the trees, I zoomed up a couple of hundred feet to see what I was doing, and pulled the bomb-release handle ...

And then I don't know what happened. Rising instantly above the *clang* of my bomb there came a roar like the ending of the world. Something kicked at the tail of my SE, lifting it up as if it were paper, throwing the nose down into an almost vertical dive, out of control ...

I know that what I am describing sounds incredible, but I also know that it happened, and that men in the Squadron, Gilly amongst others, saw the machine afterwards and can testify as to its condition.

To estimate how long that dive lasted is beyond my powers. Perhaps it was two seconds, probably less. Reckoning that I was travelling at over 100 miles an hour and that when the dive started I was 200 feet up, it *must* have been less. And yet I had time for coherent thought. No past life flashed before me; my eyes remained open and it was the immediate future I looked into. I saw the ground appallingly close, coming up at dreadful speed. I felt the control stick rigid in my hand, as hard back as I could get it – but jammed! I thought that I was 'for it'. In those infinite fractions of time I passed, through fear, beyond despair into a bleak region where without hope I *knew* that I was going to dive into the ground.

And I did!

That's the extraordinary part about it. I hit the earth and survived! The machine had come slowly and almost of her own accord out of the vertical, past forty-five degrees; but she was still descending steeply and at great speed when she smashed into the earth. There was a ghastly noise of breaking and splintering, I was flung forward against the safety-belt, my head hit the windscreen; but the machine quivered, bounced, and went on – minus her undercarriage! There must have been a slight fall in the ground just there, for had it been level or sloping up I would have crashed irremediably and fatally. As it was the machine seemed to stagger forward, her speed reduced almost to stalling-point; gradually the nose came up until she hovered along a few feet from the ground. She could still fly; by some tiny fraction of time and distance she had missed stopping altogether.

And now fear returned like pain after an operation. Dead certainty of the end had acted as an anaesthetic, returning hope brought new terror. What would happen next? The control stick was impossibly heavy, stiff, something had gone wrong with the tail. I glanced over my shoulder, and sat aghast at what I saw. On one side the fuselage had been stripped bare of its tail-plane and elevator, which now trailed, broken and tattered, at the end of a bracing-wire. The rudder was partially jammed by the wreckage; I could scarcely steer, dared not use too much force on the rudder-bar. The undercarriage, I knew, was gone, but worse than that the tip of a propeller-blade had been carried away. The engine vibration alone was nerve-shattering, and heaven knows what other damage must have been done to the framework of the machine. The extraordinary thing was that she flew at all, for the moment that was all I cared about, and the first thing to prevent was a final landing in that German territory which I had just bumped so hard.

By careful manipulation of the engine throttle and of the half-jammed control stick I succeeded in obtaining more or less level flight at an altitude of about 100 feet. Lateral control was not too bad, but with only half a tail the machine had a horrible tendency to pitch uncontrollably. The best speed, I found, was about 80 miles an hour, and to obtain this I had to run the engine at three-quarters of full throttle, thereby bringing on such a vibration as made me fear the engine would break loose if I did not land soon. But land in German territory I refused to do. Somehow I still had a greater horror of recapture than of the probable results of a crash.

And the likelihood of a crash was brought home to me by the attitude of the enemy. I passed over a nest of German machine-gunners. I saw the gun pointed, the men in field-grey crouching behind it. But the gun did not fire. Looking down miserably at them I watched their heads rise, looked into their upturned faces, almost caught the expression of blank surprise in their open-mouthed immobility. They were too amazed at my wheelless, tailless, rattling machine to think of firing ... I overtook a solitary steel-helmeted German walking towards the front. He spun round in alarm when he heard me coming, bent down to take cover; then slowly straightened up again and stood regarding me, legs apart, hands on hips. I could almost hear his muttered '*Schweinhund Englander!*' as I passed unsteadily on my way. It was the same with the rest of them. The enemy did not think it worth their while to waste ammunition on a doomed and harmless craft.

I had been heading almost due north at the moment of the explosion and, although I could not see much of the country when I came out of the dive, I knew enough to realise that I was now making for Cambrai and not for the lines. With infinite care I pressed the rudder-bar to bring the nose round from north-east, through north, to north-west. More than this I dared not attempt, for the remains of the tail were now vibrating nearly as much as the engine; greater pressure on the rudder might bring about a final collapse. But in a little while, clearing some tree-tops by a few feet, I saw the Scheldt Canal go by beneath me. It was the first reassuring sign since the crash and it gave me confidence to continue, though by now I was as frightened of coming down as of staying up, knowing that I would have practically no control of the machine on landing.

Then I began to see the *backs* of Germans in trenches, in shell-holes, behind mounds and in the ruins of houses. The earth started to spout broken fountains of mud, earth, stones, cement even. Clouds of sulphurous smoke rolled by, whilst above the banging of my engine I could hear the deep shuddering boom of guns. The crippled machine wobbled about perilously in the disturbed air, so that at times I thought all control must be lost. It took an age to cross the battle-zone; I wondered what would happen if I came down in the midst of it. Where was the front and where the British lines? Looking over the side, I tried to judge from the direction of the enemy's fire as to which way I should turn, if turn I could. And all at once I noticed that I was getting much lower. Less than 50 feet from the ground. More like twenty. I tried to climb a little. Impossible. The machine lost speed at once ... '*Courage,*' *he cried, and pointed toward the land* – good fellow Tennyson, but where was his *mounting wave* to roll me *shoreward*? Ah – I had it. I was not coming lower, it was the ground rising. There was a hill ahead of me – a well-known hill, wood, village: Bourlon! Our people had attacked it that same morning. Question was, had they taken it? If so, I might be safe yet ... The ground came closer. In a few more seconds I would have to crash.

I began to see faces, not backs, in the trenches and shell-holes. Dimly through the smoke I distinguished khaki uniforms. The shell-fire was less heavy. Ahead a gun flashed in my face, firing in the direction whence I had come. The ground drew still nearer, so near that had I possessed an under-carriage the wheels would already have been rolling upon the pitted earth where dead men lay as well in khaki as in field grey. I tried to pull the nose up, got the speed to just below eighty. Switched off, slithered along the ground, hit the rim of a small crater. There was a final crashing and splintering, from the wings this time, and the machine burying her engine in the ground thumped over on to her back.

And then, as the saying is, everything went dark.

*   *   *

When I came to, a few seconds later. I was being hauled out of the wreck-age by a couple of burly private soldiers. An officer with a very red face stood by, directing operations as though he were assisting at a rather un-interesting bit of salvage work.

'Blimey, sir,' said one of them, 'look at all the berlood!'

That remark brought me round. I was sure it must be serious, although I could feel nothing but a few bruises. The officer hurried forward solicitously.

'Are you wounded?'

Then if ever I should have quoted Browning: 'Not wounded, Sire, but dead!' I was too slow. It was the private soldier who answered for me.

'Garn, sir, it's only 'is nose what's bleedin'!' And when I thought of all my recent anxieties, it seemed a lot of trouble to have been at to get so little …

The place where I had landed (in a manner of speaking) had been captured an hour previously, so that I had timed my descent rather well. The hill-side was no longer under rifle fire, and the fact that it was being shelled at odd intervals was not sufficient to deter the rank and file; a crowd of idlers soon collected such as, in peace time, assemble to watch Oxford Street being taken up. Through the midst of them there hurried presently a dapper gunner subaltern. He clicked his heels and flung me a salute that would have shamed the Guards at Buckingham Palace. 'Battery-commander's compliments, sir, and if you wish for assistance we shall be happy to do anything in our power.' He saluted again.

'Thanks awfully,' I said, holding my nose and feeling very giddy. But why the 'sir' business and all this saluting? It had been a warm day and I was not wearing flying-kit over my tunic. I saw him glance down in a puzzled manner at the badges on my sleeve, and when he spoke again it was in a much less humble tone.

'Oh – I thought you were at least a Wing Commander. You had such a very big streamer on your machine.'

'Streamer be blowed!' said I. 'That was my tailplane.'

I went on to tell him of some of the peculiar things which had befallen me, thinking that being a gunner he might be able to find an explanation for my having been blown up. But he was listless from the start and at the end plainly disappointed.

'The Battery-commander thought you were flying a new type of machine – very fast, without the wheels, don't you know ...'

I left him gazing at my wrecked aeroplane, and walked back to the balloon line, where they gave me a much-needed whisky-and-soda. Then, finding a tender returning empty to the depot, I hopped on board and was driven back to the Squadron.

CHAPTER FOUR

EXPLOITS OF THE ESCAPING CLUB

By J. Evans

In the early days of the War Fort 9, Ingolstadt, had been a quiet, well-behaved sort of place, according to its oldest inmates. But for the six months previous to my arrival before its forbidding gates at the end of 1916, the Germans had collected into it all the naughty boys who had tried to escape from other camps. There were about 150 officer prisoners of different nationalities in the place, and at least 130 of these had successfully broken out of other camps, and had only been recaught after from three days' to three weeks' temporary freedom. I myself had escaped from Clausthal in the Harz Mountains – but had been recaptured on the Dutch frontier after I'd been at large for a few days.

When I arrived at Fort 9, Ingolstadt, 75 per cent of the prisoners were scheming and working continually to escape again. Escaping, and how it should be done, was the most frequent subject of conversation. In fact, the camp was nothing less than an escaping club. We pooled our knowledge and each man was ready to help anyone who wished to escape, quite regardless of his own risk or the punishment he might bring upon himself. No one cared two pence for court-martials, and nearly everyone in the fort had done considerable spells of solitary confinement.

It is scarcely necessary to say that the Germans, having herded some 150 officers with the blackest characters into one camp, took considerable precautions to keep them there. But there were some of the most ingenious people in Fort 9 that I've ever met – particularly among the French – and attempts to escape took place at least once a week.

Fort 9 had been built in 1866 after the Austrian wars. There was a wide moat, about 15 yards broad and 5 feet deep, round the whole fort and inside the moat the ramparts rose to a height of 40 feet. Our living rooms were actually in the ramparts and the barred windows looked down upon the moat, across a grass path along which a number of sentries were posted. It looked as though there were only two possible ways of getting out: to go out the way we'd come in, past three sentries, three gates and a guardhouse; or to swim the moat. It was impossible to tunnel under the moat. It had been tried, and the water came into the tunnel as soon as it got below the water level. An aeroplane seemed the only other solution. That was the problem we were up against, and however you look at it, it always boiled down to a nasty cold swim or a colossal piece of bluff. We came to the conclusion that we must have more accurate knowledge of the numbers, positions and movements of the sentries on the ramparts and round the moat at night, so we decided that one of us must spend the night out. It would be a rotten job; fifteen hours' wait on a freezing night, for it was now winter. For the first three and last three hours of this time it would be almost impossible to move a muscle without discovery, and discovery probably meant getting bayoneted. We cast lots for this job – and it fell to a man named Oliphant. I owned I breathed a sigh of relief. There would be two roll-calls to be faked, the roll-call just before sunset and the early morning one. How was this to be done? Our room was separated from the one next door, which was occupied by Frenchmen, by a 3-foot thick wall, and in the wall was an archway. This archway was boarded up and formed a recess which was used as a hanging cupboard for clothes. Under cover of these clothes we cut a hole in the boarding big enough for a man to slip quickly through from one room to the other. The planks which we took out could be put back easily and we pasted pictures over the cracks to conceal them. It was rather difficult work. We had only a heated table knife to cut the first plank with, but later on we managed to steal a saw from a German carpenter, who was doing some work in one of the rooms, and return it before he missed it. You must remember that there was absolutely no privacy in the fort, and a sentry passed the window and probably stared into the room every minute or two. We then rehearsed the faking of the roll-calls. One of us pretended to be the German NCO taking the roll. First he tapped at the Frenchman's door and counted the men in the room, shut the door and walked about seven paces to our door, tapped and entered. Between the time he shut the first door till he opened ours only six or eight seconds elapsed, but during these seconds one of the Frenchmen had to slip through the hole, put on a British warm, and pretend to be Oliphant; the German NCOs knew every man by sight in every room, but so long as the numbers were correct they often didn't bother to examine our faces. That accounted for the evening roll-call. The early morning one was really easier. For several mornings the fellow in bed nearest the hole in our room made a habit of covering his face with the bedclothes. The German NCO soon got used to seeing him like that, and if he saw him breathing or moving didn't bother to pull the clothes off his face. So the Frenchman next door had simply to jump out of bed as soon as he had been counted, slip through the hole, and into the bed in our room, and cover up his face. We practised this until we got it perfect, and the rehearsals were great fun.

The next thing to do was to hide Oliphant on the ramparts. Two of us dug a grave for him there while the others kept watch. Then just before the roll-call went we buried him and covered him with sods of grass. It was freezing at the time. It was about 4.30pm when we buried him, and he wouldn't be able to return to our room till 8.15 the next morning, when the doors were open. The faking of the evening roll-call went off splendidly, but the morning one was a little ticklish, as we couldn't be quite sure which room the NCO would enter first. However, we listened carefully, and fixed it all right, and when he poked our substitute, who groaned and moved in the rehearsed manner, we nearly died with suppressed laughter. About an hour later Oliphant walked in very cold and hungry but otherwise cheerful. He had had quite a successful night. A bright moon had prevented him from crawling about much, but he had seen enough to show that it would be a pretty difficult job to get through the sentries and swim the moat on a dark night. However, Providence came to our help.

The winter of 1916 was a hard one, and the moat froze over, and although the Germans went round in a boat every day and tried to keep the ice broken, they eventually had to give it up. It was difficult to know whether the ice would bear or not, but I tested it as well as I could by throwing stones on to it, and decided one morning that I would risk it and make a dash across the moat that evening. A man named Wilkin, and Kicq, a little Belgian officer, who had accompanied me on my previous attempt to escape, agreed to come with me.

Our plan was to start when the 'appell' or roll-call bell went at 5.00pm, for it got dark soon afterwards, and I trusted that this would cover our flight. We had to run down a steep bank on to the ice, about 40 yards across the ice, and then another 200 yards or so before we could put a cottage between ourselves and the sentries. There was sure to be some shooting, but we reckoned the men's hands would be very cold, for they would already have been two hours at their posts. Moreover they were only armed with old French rifles, which they handled badly. We arranged with some of the other officers to create a diversion when the roll-call bell went by yelling and throwing stones on to the ice to distract the attention of the two nearest sentries. Our main anxiety was: would the ice bear? I felt confident it would. Wilkin said he was awfully frightened, but would go on with it. Kicq said that if I was confident, so was he. It would be extremely unpleasant if the ice broke, for we would be wearing a lot of very heavy clothes. Still, anyone who thinks too much of what may happen will never escape from prison. We filled our rucksacks with rations for a ten days' march and enough solidified alcohol for at least one hot drink a day. We then concealed them and our coats at the jumping-off place.

A few minutes before the bell went we were all three dressed and in our places. It was a bad few minutes. At last it rang and almost immediately I heard laughter and shouting and the sound of stones falling on the ice. We jumped up and bolted over the path and down the slope. I was slightly ahead of the others, and when I got to the moat I gave a little jump on to the ice, thinking that if it was going to break at all it would break at the edge instead of in the middle. It didn't break, and I shuffled across at good speed. When I was about half-way over I heard furious yells of 'Halt!' behind me, followed by a fair amount of shooting; but I was soon up the bank on the far side and through a few scattered trees. Then I looked back.

The others were only just clambering up the bank from the moat, and were a good 100 yards behind me. It turned out that instead of taking a little jump on to the ice as I had done, they'd stepped carefully on to the edge, which had broken under their weight, and they had fallen flat on their faces. Wilkin had somehow got upside down, his heavy rucksack falling over his head, so that he couldn't move, but Kicq had freed himself and pulled Wilkin out.

The covering parties had done their job well. They'd managed to divert the attention of the most formidable sentry until I was well on the ice. He had then noticed me, yelled 'Halt!' loaded his rifle as fast as possible, dropped on one knee, fired and missed. Cold fingers, abuse and some stones hurled at him by the party on the ramparts above had not helped to steady his aim. After one or two shots his rifle jammed. Yells and cheers from the spectators. He tore at the bolt, cursing and swearing, and then put up his rifle at the crowd of jeering prisoners above him, but they could see that the bolt hadn't gone home, and only yelled louder.

Meanwhile, I'd nearly reached the cottage, when I saw a large, four-horse wagon on the main road on my right with a number of civilians by it. They were only about 150 yards away, and they started after us, led by a strong, healthy-looking fellow with a cart-whip. The going through the snow was heavy, especially with the weight we were carrying; so the carter quickly overtook me and slashed me across the shoulders with his whip. I turned and rushed at him, but he jumped out of my reach. His companions then arrived, and I saw, too, some armed soldiers coming on bicycles along the road from the fort. The game was up, and the next thing to do was to avoid being shot in the excitement of re-capture. So I beckoned the smallest man and said in German: 'Come here, and I'll give myself up to you.' The chap with the whip immediately came forward. 'No, not to you,' I said, 'you hit me with that whip.' The little fellow was very pleased, for there was a 100 marks reward for the capture of an officer, so he hung on to my coat-tails as we started back to the fort. I tore up my map and dropped it into a stream as we went.

The scene in the Commandant's office was quite amusing. We were stripped and searched. I had nothing more to hide, but both Kicq and Wilkin had compasses, which they smuggled through with great skill. Kicq's was hidden in the lining of his greatcoat, and Wilkin had his in his handkerchief, which he pulled out of his pocket and waved to show that there was nothing in it. All our foodstuffs and clothes were returned to us, except my tin of solidified alcohol. I protested, but in vain. I was given a receipt for it and told I could have it back at the end of the war. As we left the office I saw it standing almost within my reach, and nearly managed to pocket it as I went out. However, I found a friend of mine – a French officer – outside and explained to him the position of the tin and suggested that he should go in with a few pals and steal it back for me under the cover of a row. This was the kind of joke that the Frenchmen loved, and they were past-masters at it. They were always rushing off to the Commandant's office with frivolous complaints about one thing and another, just for a rag, which never failed to reduce the Commandant and his officers to a state of dithering rage. Within ten minutes I had my solid alcohol back all right, and kept my receipt for it as well.

Compasses and maps were, of course, forbidden, but we managed to get them smuggled out in parcels all the same and watching a German open a parcel in which you knew there was a concealed compass was one of the most exciting things I've ever done.

For the next six weeks life was rather hard. It froze continuously, even in the daytime, and at night the thermometer registered more than 27 degrees of frost. Fuel and light shortage became very serious. We stole wood and coal freely from the Germans, and although the sentries had strict orders to shoot at sight anyone seen taking wood, nearly all the wood work in the fort was eventually torn down and burnt.

The Germans didn't allow us much oil for our lamps, so we used to steal the oil out of the lamps in the passage, until the Germans realised that they were being robbed and substituted acetylene for oil. However, this didn't deter us, for now, instead of taking the oil out of the lamps, we took the lamps themselves, and lamp-stealing became one of the recognised sports of the camp. How it was done has nothing to do with escaping, but was amusing. Outside our living rooms there was a passage 70 yards long, in which were two acetylene lamps. The sentry in the passage had special orders, a loaded rifle and fixed bayonet, to see that these lamps weren't stolen, and since the feldwebel, or sergeant-major, had stuffed up the sentries with horrible stories about our murderous characters, it isn't surprising that each sentry was very keen to prevent us stealing the lamps and leaving him – an isolated German – in total darkness and at our mercy. So whenever a prisoner came out of his room and passed one of the lamps, the sentry would eye him anxiously and get ready to charge at him. The lamps were about 30 yards apart, and this is how we got them. One of us would come out, walk to a lamp and stop beneath it. This would unnerve the sentry, who would advance upon him. The prisoner would then take out his watch and look at it by the light of the lamp, as if that were all he had stopped for. Meanwhile a second officer would come quickly out of a room further down the passage and take down the other lamp behind the sentry's back. The sentry would immediately turn and charge with loud yells of: 'Halt! Halt!' whereupon the first lamp would also be grabbed, both would be blown out simultaneously, and the prisoners would disappear into their respective rooms leaving the passage in total darkness. The amusing part was that this used to happen every night, and the sentries *knew* it was going to happen, but they were quite powerless against tactics of this kind.

At about this time an officer named Medlicott and I learnt that some Frenchmen were trying to escape across the frozen moat by cutting a window-bar in the latrines which overlooked it. The Germans, however, smelt a rat, but though they inspected the bars carefully they couldn't find the cuts which had been artfully sealed up with a mixture of flour and ashes. Then the feldwebel went round and shook each bar violently in turn until the fourth one came off in his hands and he fell down flat on his back. They then wired up the hole, but Medlicott and I saw a chance of cutting the wire and making another bolt for it about a week later, and we took it. We were only at large however for about two hours. The snow on the ground gave our tracks away; we were pursued, surrounded, and eventually had to surrender again. This time we had a somewhat hostile reception when we got back to the fort.

They searched us and took away my tin of solidified alcohol again. They recognised it. 'I know how you stole this back,' said the senior clerk as he gave me another receipt for it, 'but you shan't have it any more.' We both laughed over it. I laughed last, however, as I stole it back again in about a week's time, and kept my two receipts for it as well.

It may seem extraordinary that we weren't punished severely for these attempts to escape, but there were no convenient cells in which to punish us. All the cells at Fort 9 were always full and there was a very long waiting list besides.

After this failure I joined some Frenchmen who were making a tunnel. The shaft was sunk in the corner of one of their rooms close to the window, and the idea was to come out in the steep bank of the moat on a level with the ice and crawl over on a dark night. It was all very unpleasant. Most of the time one lay in a pool of water and in an extremely confined space and worked in pitch darkness, as the air was so bad that no candle would keep alight. Moreover, when we got close to the frozen surface of the ground it was always a question whether the sentry outside wouldn't put his foot through the tunnel, and if he did so whether one would be suffocated or stuck with a bayonet. It was most unpleasant lying there and waiting for him to pass within six inches of your head. All the earth had to be carried in bags along the passage and emptied down the latrines.

Unfortunately, just before the work was finished the thaw set in, and it was generally agreed that we couldn't afford to get our clothes wet swimming the moat. However, the Frenchmen were undaunted and determined to wade through the moat naked, carrying two bundles of kit sewn in waterproof cloths. The rest of us disliked the idea of being chased naked in the middle of winter carrying two twenty-pound bundles, so we decided to make ourselves diving suits out of mackintoshes. We waterproofed the worn patches of these with candle grease, and sewed them up in various places. The Frenchmen would have to fake roll-call, so they made most life-like dummies, which breathed when you pulled a string, to put in their beds. Whether this attempt to escape would have been successful I can't say, for, thank Heaven, we never tried it. When we were all ready and the French colonel, who was going first, had stripped naked and greased himself from head to foot, we learnt that the trap-door which we had made at the exit of the tunnel couldn't be opened under two hours owing to unexpected roots and stones. We had to put off the attempt for that night, and we were unable to make another as the end of the tunnel suddenly fell in, and the cavity was noticed by the sentry.

This was practically the end of my residence in Fort 9, for soon after the Germans decided to send the more unruly of us to other camps. We learnt that we were to be transferred to Zorndorf, in East Prussia, an intolerable spot from all accounts, and a man named Buckley and myself decided to get off the train at the first opportunity and make another bid for freedom. The train would be taking us directly away from the Swiss frontier, so it behoved us to leave it as soon as possible. We equipped ourselves as well as we could with condensed foods before starting, and wore Burberrys to cover our uniforms. Although there were only thirty of us going we had a guard of an officer and fifteen men, which we thought a little excessive. We had two hours' wait at the station and amused ourselves by taking as little notice as possible of the officer's orders, which annoyed him and made him shout. Six of us and a sentry were then packed rather tightly into a second-class carriage. We gave him the corner seat next to the corridor, and another sentry marched up and down the corridor outside. Buckley and I took the seats by the window, which we were compelled to keep closed, and there was no door in that side of the carriage. The position didn't look very hopeful, for there wasn't much chance of our sentry going to sleep with the other one outside continually looking in. Just before we started the officer came fussing in: he was obviously very anxious and nervous, and said he hoped that we would have a comfortable, quiet journey and no more trouble. The train started, night fell, and the frontier was left further and further behind. We shut our eyes for an hour to try to induce the sentry to go to sleep, but this didn't work.

The carriage was crowded, and both racks were full of small luggage, and, noticing this, I had an idea. I arranged with the others to act in a certain way when the train next went slowly, and I gave the word by saying to the sentry, in German: 'Will you have some food? We are going to eat.' Five or ten minutes of tense excitement followed. Suddenly the train began to slow up. I leant across and said to the sentry, 'Will you have some food? We are going to eat.' Immediately everyone in the carriage stood up with one accord and pulled their stuff off the racks. The sentry also stood up, but was almost completely hidden from the window by a confused mass of men and bags. Under cover of this confusion, Buckley and I stood up on our seats. I slipped the strap of my haversack over my shoulder, pushed down the window, put my leg over and jumped into the night. I fell – not very heavily – on the wires at the side of the track, and lay still in the dark shadow. Three seconds later Buckley came flying out after me, and seemed to take rather a heavy toss. The end of the train wasn't yet past me, and we knew there was a man with a rifle in the last carriage; so when Buckley came running along the track calling out to me, I caught him and pulled him into the ditch at the side. The train went by, and its tail lights vanished round a corner and apparently no one saw or heard us.

I have not space to say much about our walk to the German-Swiss frontier, about 200 miles away. We only walked by night, and lay up in hiding all through the hours of daylight which was, I think, the worst part of the business and wore out our nerves and physical strength far more than the six or seven hours marching at night, for the day seemed intolerably long from 4.30am to 9.30pm – seventeen hours – the sun was very hot, and there was little shade, and we were consumed with impatience to get on. Moreover, we could never be free from anxiety at any moment of those seventeen hours. The strain at night of passing through a village when a few lights still burnt and dogs seemed to wake and bark at us in every house, or of crossing a bridge when one expected to be challenged at any moment never worried me so much as a cart passing or men talking near our daytime hiding-places.

We went into hiding at dawn or soon after, and when we'd taken off our boots and put on clean socks we would both drop asleep at once. It was a bit of a risk – perhaps one of us ought to have stayed awake, but we took it deliberately since we got great benefit from a sound sleep while we were still warm from walking. And it was only about an hour before we woke again shivering, for the mornings were very cold and we were usually soaked with dew up to our waists. Then we had breakfast – the great moment of the day – and rations were pretty good at first, as we underestimated the time we would take by about four days. But later on we had to help things out with raw potatoes from the fields, which eventually became our mainstay. All day long we were pestered with stinging insects. Our hands and faces became swollen all over, and the bites on my feet came up in blisters which broke and left raw places when I put on my boots again.

On the fifteenth day our impatience got the better of us, and we started out before it was properly dark, and suddenly came upon a man in soldier's uniform scything grass at the side of the road. We were filthily dirty and unshaven and must have looked the most villainous tramps; it was stupid of us to have risked being seen; but it would have aroused his suspicion if we'd turned back, so we walked on past him. He looked up and said something we didn't catch. We answered: 'Good evening' as usual. But he called after us, and then when we took no notice, shouted: 'Halt! Halt!' and ran after us with his scythe.

We were both too weak to run fast or far, and moreover we saw at that moment a man with a gun about 50 yards to our right. There was only one thing to be done, and we did it. We turned haughtily and waited for our pursuer, and when he was a few yards away Buckley demanded in a voice quivering with indignant German what the devil he meant by shouting at us. He almost dropped his scythe with astonishment, then turned round and went slowly back to his work. Buckley had saved the day.

The end of our march on the following night brought us within 15 kilometres of the Swiss frontier, and we decided to eat the rest of our food and cross the next night. However, I kept back a few small meat lozenges. We learnt the map by heart so as to avoid having to strike matches later on, and left all our spare kit behind us in order to travel light for this last lap. But it wasn't to be our last lap.

We were awfully weak by now and made slow progress through the heavy going, and about two hours after we'd started a full bright moon rose which made us feel frightfully conspicuous. Moreover, we began to doubt our actual position, for a road we'd expected to find wasn't there. However, we tramped on by compass and reached a village which we hoped was a place named Riedheim, within half a mile of the frontier. But here we suddenly came on a single line railway which wasn't on our map. We were aghast – we were lost – and moreover Buckley was fearfully exhausted for want of food, so we decided to lie up for another night in a thick wood on a hill. The meat lozenges I'd saved now came in very handy and we also managed to find water and some more raw potatoes. Then we slept, and when daylight came studied our small scale map and tried to make head or tail of our situation.

We had a good view of the countryside from our position but could make nothing of it. Perhaps we were already in Switzerland? It was essential to know and it was no good looking for signposts since they'd all been removed within a radius of 10 miles of the frontier. I think we were both slightly insane by now from hunger and fatigue; anyhow I decided to take a great risk. I took off my tunic and walking down into the fields asked a girl who was making hay what the name of the village was. It was Riedheim – as I'd originally thought. The railway of course had been made after the map was printed. I don't know what the girl thought of my question and appearance; she gave me a sly look, but went on with her work. I returned to Buckley, and when it was quite dark we left our hiding-place. We had three-quarters of an hour to cross the frontier before the moon rose – and we had to go with the greatest care. For a time we walked bent double, and then we went down on our hands and knees, pushing our way through the thick long grass of water meadows. The night was so still – surely the swishing of the grass as we moved through it must be audible for hundreds of yards. On and on we went – endlessly it seemed – making for a stream which we had seen from our hill and now knew must be the boundary line. Then the edge of the moon peered at us over the hills. We crawled at top speed now, until Buckley's hand on my heel suddenly brought me to a halt. About 15 yards ahead was a sentry. He was walking along a footpath on the bank of a stream. *The* stream. He had no rifle, and had probably just been relieved. He passed without seeing us. One last spurt and we were in the stream and up the other bank. 'Crawl,' said Buckley. 'Run,' said I, and we ran. It was just after midnight when we crossed into Switzerland and freedom on our eighteenth night out.

CHAPTER FIVE

HOODWINKING THE GERMANS

By Lieutenant Anselme Marchal

After my release from the civilian prison of Magdeburg, I was sent back to Scharnhorst, the most rigorous prison camp in Germany. A little later, towards the end of December, 1917, a new companion in captivity was given, or rather returned, to me. It was Roland Garros.

He and I had been imprisoned together before, but separated because we had refused to answer the incessant roll-calls with which we were plagued and had incited the rest of the prisoners to do the same. Garros had been confined in the camp of Burg, but now all French officers were being evacuated from Burg in order to make room for the Russian officers who were being concentrated there. Germany and Russia were making the peace of Brest-Litovsk, so it had been decided to prevent any contact between our wavering allies and ourselves.

After Burg, Garros was at first transferred to the Wagenhaus with the French officers who were not undergoing reprisals. He was kept there for about two weeks. At the end of that time a search proved him to be the possessor of the important sum of 2 marks in German money and a pair of pincers. It needed no more to earn him a few days' confinement in the cells. Afterwards, as penance for his two crimes, he was sent to Scharnhorst.

I found in Garros the good friend of peace-times, who had always had my affection, and the great pilot of war-times, who had as yet been prevented by circumstances from giving his full measure.

The close intimacy in which we lived at Scharnhorst and the trials we were soon to undergo together could not do otherwise than transform our former good-comradeship into the deepest of affections. Nobody could be admitted to the intimacy of Garros's mind without feeling respect and admiration for his very superior intelligence, nor into the intimacy of his heart without loving him.

*   *   *

As soon as we found ourselves together again at Scharnhorst, we 'pooled' all the different projects or escapes that he and I had imagined. Garros had only one idea – to escape and take his revenge. Before six weeks were out we had found a possible way of getting out of the camp.

When I first came to Scharnhost I talked freely of my intention to escape. One day a Russian officer came to me with a most engaging air, saying how much he deplored the lack of success of my previous attempt, and offering to help me in a new effort, all this being seasoned with so many compliments on my coolness and courage as to put me well on my guard. Finally, he bluntly offered to take me to a room of which he had the key, and from which he assured me I could escape into the moat without being seen.

While I had few illusions as to the sincerity of this most devoted of Russians, I took him at his word and let him show me the little room he had described. Once there I had only to put an eye to the window to assure myself that it would be impossible to find a less promising place. At 10 metres' distance was silhouetted the grey form of a sentinel, and as he would undoubtedly be given very good reasons for being on his guard, it is easy to imagine what would have been the fate of Marchal the runaway potted at 'sitting'.

My Russian was, as you choose, either a most extraordinary imbecile or something of a dirty dog; for myself, I lean towards the second hypothesis.

After that I was more discreet, in case some other amateur Judas should try to betray me; but my constant preoccupation was how to part company with my guardians, and I did not stop examining every possible plan of escape.

Escape in the twilight, by boldly walking through one of the gates, past the sentries, still seemed to me to be the method requiring the greatest amount of assurance, but at the same time offering the greatest chance of success, as being the least expected.

Since my previous attempt I had been particularly recommended to the vigilance of the non-commissioned officers of the guard, and confronted with each one in turn, so that in future they would have no difficulty in recognising me, whatever my disguise. I had to get over this difficulty. Ever since the beginning of the winter I had never shown myself in the courtyard except wrapped up in my overcoat, the collar turned up so as to hide almost the whole of my face. As the months passed I hoped that the guard would have forgotten my face, and any way my face would have become blurred in the memories of the non-coms. Garros agreed with me that this was the best plan, and we prepared accordingly.

We would both dress up as German officers and walk boldly out of the prison.

The first thing was to fake the kits. We begged some permanganate of potash from a doctor and made a strong solution. In this we washed our two French officers' coats, until they ceased to be horizon blue and became campaign grey. The buttons we carved out of wood with penknives, and painted them greenish bronze. Out of our pilots' overalls we got enough fur to make collars for the coats.

One of our friends made us caps. They were a great success. He made the frames out of pieces of cardboard from a box. The tops he covered with blue cloth cut out of a pair of trousers, and then made bands out of a red-flannel belt. This he stole from an old colonel who wore it at night. We hoped the poor old man would not catch a chill. With some nickel he made cockades such as the Germans carried on their caps; and no one at a distance, or in a bad light, could have told them from the real thing. They were 'creations'.

We cut down some slats of wood into the shape of sabres and blacked them over with shoe-blacking.

Garros produced two suits of civilian clothes. Goodness knows how he had kept them concealed in his trips from prison to prison. He had, however, brought them to Scharnhorst and secreted them between a wall and a wood fence where there was a loose plank. The Germans never knew where those civilian suits came from, and I cannot tell. I don't know.

The hardest task was to forge false passes with false names. I knew German and Germany well, for I had lived there and travelled in the country before the war, and I managed these pretty successfully after several tries.

* * *

As the date we had chosen arrived we got the assistance of our comrades. There were none of the 'amateur Judases' among them. They worked for us like blacks, and they gave us all their assistance loyally. Two other officers – Captain Meyer and Lieutenant Gille – also determined to escape, but were prepared to let us get away first.

It was important to keep our escape concealed as long as possible, so as to give us a good start. We intended to go as dusk came, so the evening roll-call was the first problem. We devised a complicated plan.

Garros and I were in Room 7 in the right wing of the Scharnhorst on the first floor. A wooden partition that divided the casement in two separated us from Room 8. A trap-door had been made in this partition, by means of which two of our comrades from No. 8 proposed to pass at the opportune moment and replace us in No. 7. But on reflection our friends decided that the proximity of the two rooms would not allow the substitution, however rapidly carried out, to be made in the too-short time that it would take the inspecting officer of the week to reach the second room after having assured himself that the first had its full number of occupants. So it was decided to ask two French officers of Room II, also situated on the first floor, but in the left wing of the bastion, to come and occupy Garro's and my beds when the non-commissioned officer of the week had visited their room and had been able to announce to his lieutenant '*Alles da!*' ('Everything there').

This time, in order that no absences should be remarked from Room II, it was essential that our two substitutes should be found in it when the officer came, condemned though they were to spend the whole night in No. 7. They were found there, if not in person, at least in the shape of two friends from Room 15 on the second floor, which was situated immediately over theirs. Lieutenant Chalon, our renowned engineer in the Scharnhorst, cut a hole through the solid masonry of Room 15 down into Room 11 and concealed it. As soon as we were gone our two friends from No. 11 would come to No. 7 and get into our beds. The two from No. 15 on the second floor would drop through the hole in the floors and take the place of the two who should have been in No. 11. As soon as the German officer had inspected No. 11 and started up the staircase to the second floor they were to be hoisted up again into their own room by main force, so that by the time the Prussian officer and his NCOs had got to their room they would be back in their own places and the Prussians could report 'Everything there.'

The falsification of the morning roll-call, however, would not be so easy, for it was held in the open courtyard. The inmates of each room were fallen in as a group and counted, while the rooms were guarded by sentries, so that no one could go in or out.

*   *   *

The day arrived – 14 February 1918. Two of our friends kept watch in the passage, to see that we were not disturbed. Several others came to help us with our kit. We rigged ourselves out in our civilian suits and put our faked German' overcoats over them. To cover our trousers legs we had some gaiters. Then we strapped on our 'swords,' adjusted our caps to a good angle with a touch of swagger, and as complete German officers were ready.

As it began to get to twilight we marched out and up to the gate known as the Wagenhaus Gate.

Newly captured British troops headed by an officer are being escorted back from the fighting. They are being loosely guarded – a good time to slip away, as many did. The further back they got the harder it became to escape.

A group of prisoners with their unarmed guard who is obviously not expecting any problem from them.

An injured airman being helped from the crash site. As a prized prisoner there would be little chance to escape even if he was physically able.

Further back the prisoners were watched more closely. Here they are watched by two guards and a group of onlookers leaving them little chance of escape.

On arrival at the camp the number of guards increased. Here they wait to be processed behind the barbed wire of their new home.

Let into the inner camp through more gates and wire, escape would now require a lot of planning.

At regular intervals the perimeter had a watchtower; not all were as well built or protected from the weather as this one.

Officers' quarters were generally in pre-existing buildings like this new cavalry barracks that would become famous for the greatest escape of the war.

As well as the wire and gates there were always guards walking around. These are setting off to patrol the outer fence.

Conditions in other ranks' barracks were never comfortable but a stove like this in the summer could be a useful starting point for a tunnel.

Civilians were also put in camps. These are the arms of Ruhleben Internment Camp in Berlin where most British male civilians were held.

Most were healthy and relatively young. Being better fed than their enlisted military counterparts, many tried to escape; some were successful.

The accommodation provided for officers was far more comfortable. This is a communal living space.

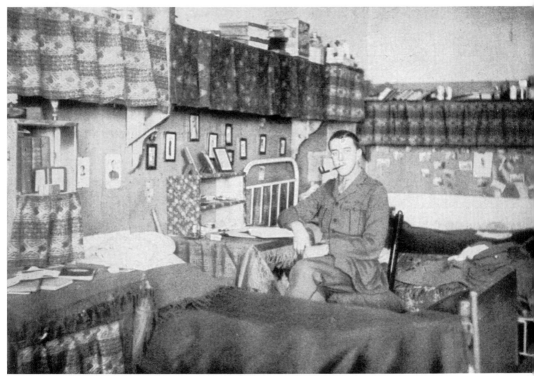

Like the men, most had to share their sleeping accommodation. This is an officer's bedroom – a perfect place to plot an escape as many did.

A failed escape tunnel that came to the surface too early.

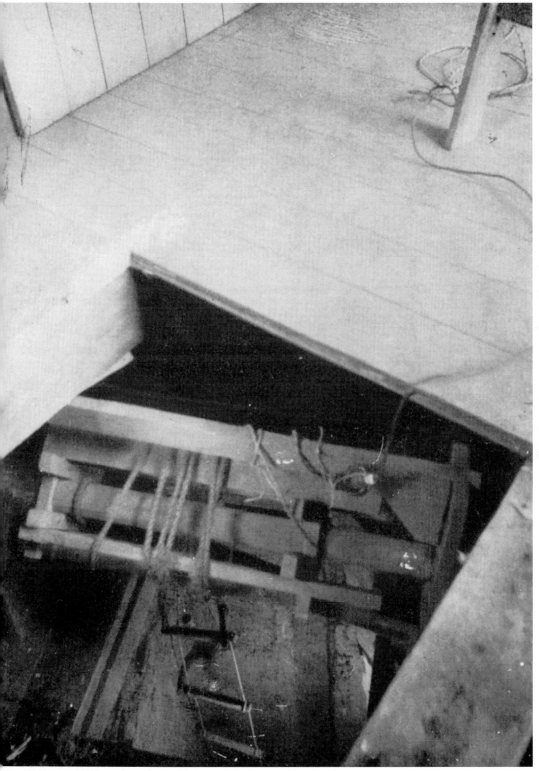
A rope ladder down to the excavation of a tunnel hidden in a disused building.

Tools confiscated by guards. They had been found in a tunnel under construction.

Escapers all, recaptured officers in a room at Holzminden. Left to right: Churchill, Lyon, Clouston, Robertson, Sharp, Bennet and Matlock.

The escape tunnel at Holzminden after its discovery.

Private food parcels were the easiest way to get escape equipment, especially if the guards were lazy and did not inspect the parcels properly. Unfortunately, this compass was discovered during an inspection.

Parcels had to wrapped in a specific way otherwise they might not get through. On arrival the camp the guards were supposed to inspect everything including the contents of tins to make smuggling more difficult.

The typical contents of a parcel. Bread could be baked with objects inside and cakes could be cooked with maps as tin liners.

For the lucky escape the end of the journey was unguarded. Here a static guard is talking to a mounted guard who rode along the frontier.

In many places the fence was electrified. The sign on the wire between Belgium and Holland read 'Warning! High Voltage. Danger to Life' with a guard house behind in case anyone successfully crossed the wires.

Officers looking at a Belgian who was electrocuted trying to get to Holland.

German guards using an insulated hook to remove a cat that touched the wire.

Harry Beaumont.

Hugh Durnford taken in 1918 at Stralsund Camp from where he escaped.

Duncan Grinnell-Milne.

A.J. Evans of the escaping club.

We were a little behind our schedule and the twilight had already turned to darkness. Garro's watch – I no longer had one – marked ten minutes to six, and the train we wanted to catch left Magdeburg at half-past six. There was no time to be lost, and we lost none.

Approaching the first sentry I put on my most impressive voice and roared at Garros that it was insufferable that a German colonel should be whistled after and hooted at by the prisoners, and that it was our duty to go immediately to the general and ask him to take energetic measures to bring those insolent Frenchmen back into the paths of virtue.

The first sentry heard my words very plainly. His attitude was proof enough of that. Without uttering a syllable he drew aside, and stood at attention.

We arrived before the second. He asked us, in a timid voice, some question that I did not catch. Was it a password he wanted? If such a word existed, it would be the only one that we were quite incapable of uttering. I made good anything that may have been lacking in our reply by the crescendo in which I continued my fierce invectives against the disgraceful Franzosen who were making the life of the camp commandant a misery to him. It was time that a stop was put to such a monstrous state of affairs. Garros agreed energetically by a sort of hoarse growling. Our tactics were successful. The sentry opened the great gates and let us through.

A little farther along another sentry guarded the barbed-wire barrier that had been laid across the slope leading up to the gates. But this third guard considered himself to be covered by the second, and he said nothing to us. He stood to attention, and then saluted and opened the barrier for us.

We had now reached the footbridge over the moat. Before it was a sentry, who demanded to see our passes. Although we had them in our pockets we preferred not to show them unless it was absolutely necessary. In my most terrible voice I roared an emphatic, 'Mind your own affairs!' at him, and added, 'That makes the third time we've been asked for those damned papers!' and we brushed past, and he made no further attempt to stop us.

We walked in step slowly across that bridge, and even more slowly into the darkness beyond it, our hearts in our mouths, expecting at any minute to hear some pursuit, some of the sentries or the guard after us.

As soon as we judged we were clear and out of sight we hurried to the edge of a railway track, and in a broad ditch we crouched while we tore off our overcoats, our leggings, the officers' caps, our wooden swords, and, hiding them in a drain, we turned into peaceful German citizens. Garros had a soft felt hat and I a most disreputable cloth cap. Sticking these on our heads, we made back to the road and walked with the utmost non-chalance to Magdeburg and into the railway station.

We hoped that we had a good start. Later we heard that everything had worked well. The German officer inspecting at the evening roll-call had not noticed our absence, though our two friends from No. 15 had only been hauled back up from No. 11 just in time. Though out of breath and covered with dust they bamboozled the guards successfully. The morning roll-call had also been successful. Garros's absence was missed. A friend from our room put on his pilot's leather coat, turned the fur collar up to his eyes as was Garros's habit, and took his place in the ranks. The 'dancing master' on duty that day was oblivious to this masquerade; but not seeing me in the group, and hearing that I had reported sick, he sent up to No. 7 to question the non-com. especially detailed to watch me.

The man – who was known to us as Bismarck – came into the room, where he found only one officer, whose head and shoulders he was unable to see, their owner being busily occupied in searching for some unknown object under my bed. Without changing his position the officer in question addressed a few words of German to Bismarck, which sufficed to reassure him, as I was the only occupant of No. 7 able to speak to him in his own language.

The officer who pretended to be myself was Lieutenant Buel, who knew a little German. How he found a substitute for himself and bluffed Bismarck and the sentries I don't know. It is a mystery I have never been able to fathom, for if any prisoner for any reason did not fall in on morning roll-call his room was specially guarded by a sentry, with strict orders to see that no one went in or out.

None the less, the result was that we got a good twenty-four hours' start, and it was not until the following evening roll-call that the Germans spotted that we were gone.

When they did find out there was a real blow-up. The German papers demanded that the Chancellor make new arrangements so that no other prisoners should get away. The commandant of the camp was dismissed in disgrace. We, none of us, had any sympathy with him in that. Then a whole army of Berlin secret police descended on the prison and investigated everything and everybody, but could not for the life of them find out how we had got away.

Those in themselves were good enough results, but they were not the best. The Berlin secret police officers, the *ersatz* Sherlock Holmes, not only had their trouble for nothing in so far as finding the smallest clue as to how our own escape had been managed, but they facilitated – oh, most certainly against their will! – the successful accomplishment of another.

Absorbed as they were in ransacking the rooms and searching our fellow-prisoners they neglected to keep watch over their own pockets. And the result was that Captain Meyer, who had given up to us his turn of escape, rendered to one of the detectives the sincere flattery of imitation – though he carried out his investigations more discreetly than did the German, for he relieved him of all his identity papers.

Two days later, with Lieutenant Gille, Meyer marched out of the prison. At the gates he presented the papers of the secret service officer. The doors and barred gates of the Wagenhaus opened before him and he was gone.

Staggering at this escape right under their noses, while they were in charge and investigating, the Berlin sleuth-hounds had to set out on a new inquiry, and even then found nothing, for I expect the 'tec' didn't let on that he'd had his pocket picked.

*   *   *

Meanwhile, while the officers of four different rooms were managing, with such ingenuity, to hide our absence from Scharnhtirst for a night and a morning, we were going full-steam ahead towards the north-west.

Several times we were treated as if suspicious characters. Once several peasants who were travelling in the same direction kept asking us questions of all sorts. It may just have been their native curiosity. In order to appease this curiosity, I told them that we were going to 'Brunswick to install some motors for the Swiss Company, Oerlikon'. They swallowed the story and left us in peace, and we accomplished the first day's journey without further incident.

The train deposited us in the evening at Brunswick, and that which was to carry us towards Cologne would not pass for another six hours. What to do in the meantime? We decided to kill time by walking. We started, but into the town. The night was very dark, cold and dry. We followed a sleeping street bordered by a high fence, on the other side of which was a cemetery. If only we could get into that we would be certain of finding the safest of resting-places. The opportunity was presented to us before very long; we found a loose paling, and managed to squeeze through the narrow opening.

Our only impression, in the midst of tombs surrounded by trees black and sombre in the night, was one of security – security such as only a cemetery could possibly procure for individuals in our position. A little alley led us away from the street, and, sitting down on a tomb, we began to talk in whispers.

Hours passed. It was midnight. Suddenly I felt Garros's hand grip my arm.

'Listen,' he whispered, and we both strained our ears. It was an eerie sound that we heard, indefinable, a sort of rustling, coming from where we did not know, caused by what we did not know. It seemed to draw closer – but no, it receded, stopped, and then we heard it again, approaching. It may have been only the dragging steps of some guardian making his rounds, but even that earthly explanation was not too reassuring, and the sound was not at all like that of footsteps. Whatever it was, we did not like it, and with one accord took to our heels. I do not doubt that in our undignified flight we trampled more than one flower-border, stumbled over more than one grave, tore down more than one wreath; but at last we reached the gap in the palisade and in an instant found ourselves out in the street, where no strange thing moved about.

Train time was approaching, and we went back to the station. In the second-class carriage where chance more than our own desire led us we found two officers occupying the corners on the corridor. Never was there so undesirable a meeting; yet to turn about and leave them would have been of the utmost imprudence. We were in the soup, and the best thing we could do for the moment was to stay in it. Passing before our uncomfortable travelling companions we gave them the politest of *Guten Abends*. They replied with a nod of the head.

Squeezed into the two other corners, we sat and waited for the train to pull out. The four or five minutes we had to wait seemed an eternity. Anybody in our position is invariably afflicted by the constant and painful impression that a policeman is following on his trail, scenting the escaped prisoner from afar. At Brunswick we suffered again that agonising sensation. Whoever was the individual who walked steadily up and down the platform, keeping close to our compartment and apparently never for a minute quitting it with his eye, he can flatter himself on having made us pass a most unpleasant moment ...

At last the train drew quietly out. The night passed without incident, and in the morning we found ourselves at Cologne. Feeling somewhat ashamed of my cap, I bought a hat, and then we wandered idly about the town. But in spite of the crowded streets that made it highly improbable that anybody would pay any attention to us, we were still harassed by the fear of spies. The most reassuring manner of passing the morning that we could think of was to spend it in the cathedral; we would hardly be looked for there. We went, and heard three Masses, one after the other in rapid succession.

At a certain moment my companion nudged me with his elbow. He drew my attention to two other civilians whom we had already noticed at the preceding mass, and who now seemed to have every intention of hearing the next, like ourselves. After examining them carefully out of the corner of our eyes, we felt reassured. They were probably only very pious folk, unless, like ourselves, they had taken refuge in the cathedral in order to avoid undesirable encounters.

Prudence bade us not to venture into a restaurant, so for lunch we ate some chocolate without bread, and washed it down with beer in a bar. Afterwards we bought an electric torch that we would need for our future nocturnal peregrinations. Then we sought in the darkness of a cinema the relative security that we had found in the morning under the lofty and cold roof of the cathedral.

At the fall of evening we took a workmen's train for Aix-la-Chapelle. It was crowded. The intermediary stations being as numerous as in the outskirts of Paris, the halts were very frequent. As we drew into one of them someone in our compartment cried out: 'Ah, there are the police again, watching all the exits of the station ... I wonder what it means?'

Naturally, the meaning to us was that we had been tracked and it was for our benefit that the police had been mobilised. By a coincidence that we judged to be most fortunate the train slowed down at that moment. The stop-signal was down. I whispered to Garros, 'Let's take the chance!' I opened the carriage door, and a German soldier who was standing by it said, 'What are you up to?'

'Don't you worry about that,' I said; 'we are already an hour late, and we don't want to miss the last tram.'

While I was talking Garros had jumped from the train. I followed him, and the soldier closed the carriage door behind me.

We found ourselves in the open country, close to the railway embankment. As we were not certain of the direction of Aix, we decided to steer north-west. We walked on until we reached a spot where the houses, that had been widely scattered, began to group themselves in successive and well-populated agglomerations. Obviously, the outskirts of a big town.

We knew that one of the characteristics of Aix-la-Chapelle was a wide exterior boulevard, lined with trees, and at about 8 o'clock we came out on a boulevard that answered that description.

We had a map annotated, and which we had smuggled through to us in the prison. This told us that we should turn to the right, down a street that because of the unevenness of the ground presented the peculiarity of having one pavement raised up by four steps. The boulevard led us to that street, which we entered and followed. On a signpost we were able to read

'Direction de Tivoli'. We were on the right track, so, quite sure of ourselves now, we continued along the street, which rapidly became suburban in character. We had penetrated on to the territory of Aix, but not for more than ten minutes.

Once more in the open country, we directed our course by map and compass. The compass, too, had been smuggled into the prison in a parcel of food. The weather was chilly, but dry and seasonable – far from the 15 and 20 degrees of frost from which I had suffered so cruelly during my first terrible journey in trying to escape.

Keeping off the roads as much as possible, jumping the little rivers in order to avoid having to show our passports at the bridges, throwing ourselves flat on the ground at the least alarm, we had yet managed to make some 13 or 14 kilometres by 2 o'clock in the morning. We calculated that only 2 kilometres, at the most, still separated us from the frontier.

We entered a wood. The dried leaves with which the ground was covered made a continual crackling noise under our feet which, it seemed to us, must be audible at a great distance. Fearing that it might betray us, and looking for a path on which our footsteps would make less noise, we flashed our lamp along the ground. Immediately a shrill whistle rang out. It seemed to emanate from a little cabin that we could see on a height above the woods.

Undoubtedly our light had been seen. If that cabin should prove to be a guard-house filled with soldiers set there to watch the passages over the frontier we would be pursued and perhaps caught – and taken back to Magdeburg. No! We had no intention of accepting that. Turning to the right, and without quitting the copse, we took to our heels.

After a few minutes we came out on a transversal road, which, we realised, would lead us back in the direction of Aix. But we had no choice. Above all, we must get out of that patrol and sentry infested zone. A prey to nervous apprehensions that the high stakes for which we were playing may render excusable, we felt that an enemy lurked in every shadow, ready to leap out on us. At one time we heard footsteps both behind and before us. Turning again to the left, we fled across the open fields. Ditches and unseen obstacles made traps for us in the dark. Garros tore his face and I my hands in climbing over artificial thorn hedges of barbed wire.

The alarming noises continued. Suspicious lights, quickly flashed on and off, showed here and there in the distance. All those noises and lights were not necessarily a menace to us – we knew that quite well, but were incapable of distinguishing the innocuous from the dangerous. This perhaps needs some explanation, and it is this.

In that frontier region between Germany and Holland smuggling was never at a standstill. The smugglers made signals to each other by whistling, modulating their voices to imitate the cries of all kinds of birds – somewhat after the fashion of the 'Pirates of Savannah,' an old melodrama of my childhood's days.

Optical signals were also used. Thus, in the fields, we often saw certain individuals who followed along the rail-road track, bent double under heavy loads, and who from time to time, in order to warn the others, gave short flashes of light with their electric torches. We said to ourselves that perhaps back there in the woods it was only with *maltouziers* of this kind that we had had dealings, and whose whistling was no more than an answer to what they mistook for the signal of one of their acolytes. But hardly had we conceived that comforting thought than other shadows appeared, going in the same direction along the railway track; and this time there was no doubt about it. The silhouettes were those of soldiers on patrol … The business was comic enough to watch, had it not proved to us that we ran the double risk of being pursued on sight, either as escaped prisoners or as smugglers; and once captured, there would be little choice between the two; the result for us would be the same.

In any case we were doomed to postpone our attempt to cross the frontier until the next night; and the only thing to do in the meantime was to return to Aix-la-Chapelle. We must in any case be fairly close to it, as we had been walking for three hours and must easily have covered on the return road the 13 or 14 kilometres that we had previously made in the opposite direction.

Going straight in front of us, we came to a high railway embankment under which passed the road we were following. The spot was guarded by a sentry. Like all his kind, he was provided with an electric torch, the light of which he turned full on our faces.

'Have you got your papers?'

Without any previous collaboration the same idea came simultaneously to both of us. We put on the voices and the gestures of extreme intoxication. I replied to the soldier.

'Ole man, now you jus' lissen to me … You can't 'rrest us jus' because we live at Aix … Got paid to-day, we did … Had a rousing ole beano with some of the chaps.'

'Where?'

I gave the name of a village on the outskirts of Aix, and launched out into a complicated but circumstantial description of our bacchic prowess. The sentry showed himself indulgent. He clapped us on the back in friendly fashion, and, 'Get along with you,' he said. 'Pass, but don't let me catch you around here again.' To which I answered with the profoundest conviction, 'You can count on that, ole man.'

When we reached Aix-la-Chapelle it was nearly 5 o'clock in the morning. In the street we came across a nightwatchman whose business it was to see that all doors were properly closed. I went up to him and said: 'We are strangers in town. Could you tell us of an hotel?' Doing better than merely tell us of one, he led us to it.

We had to register – using of necessity false names – and indicate the identity papers that we would be able to produce, and the information we gave on that second point was exactly the same value that we had given on the first, and we had to pay in advance, having no baggage of any kind.

The red marks that Garros had on his face from his fall in the barbed wire earned for him more than one suspicious glance, from which I also suffered by ricochet, thanks to my lacerated hands. Nevertheless, we were allowed to have our two beds, of which we stood in considerable need, after our nocturnal stroll of 25 or 30 kilometres. However, we did not linger over-long in them, fear of being denounced to the police effectually driving away all desire for a sluggish morning. By 10 o'clock we were already downstairs, and making for the front door.

The hall porter called after us in a voice that seemed to us full of curiosity: 'What! Going already?'

'Yes, yes, we are in a hurry;' and without more ado we briskly left his company.

Condemned as we were to wait for evening before again venturing out into the country, we drifted aimlessly about the streets of Aix. But our stomachs clamoured for a pittance somewhat more substantial than that with which we had so far gratified them. Since our last meal at Scharnhorst, that is to say, twice twenty-four hours, we had in all, and for all, eaten eight small tablets of chocolate – somewhat meagre fare. And now that the eighth and last tablet had disappeared we could discover no means of replenishing our larder. Unprovided with cards or food-tickets of any kind, to present ourselves anywhere either as a diner on the premises or a purchaser of comestibles would have been to denounce ourselves infallibly; if not for what we were, at least as persons whose irregular position recommended them highly to the curiosity of the police.

Good luck led us to a mechanical bar. There, at least, we thought, there could be no danger, the machine being endowed neither with eyes nor ears. We soon found out our mistake. If the machines were deaf and blind the same could not be said of the urchins detailed to watch over them. One of these, about twelve years old and as sharp as a razor, came and planted himself next to us, obviously all ears. I broke into a voluble flood of speech, and succeeded in allaying the suspicions of the young spy to such an extent that he at last left us, and went to carry on his small affairs elsewhere.

We at once prepared for a good feed, but disappointment awaited us. The only dish that was left was jellied mussels. We could do no other than resign ourselves to the inevitable and it might be better than nothing. In return for forty pfennigs the distributor produced for our benefit seven mussels on a plate. Both of us returned twice to the charge. Then we departed, having failed to lose any great proportion of our hunger, but having gained an undeniable feeling of nausea.

In default of more solid nourishment we fell back on glasses of beer, absorbed at frequent intervals during our aimless wanderings. Unfortunately, it was *Einheilsbier*, which only had the vaguest of resemblances with the good, solid beer of peace-time.

One of these pauses we made at the Theatrellatz Tavern, where Munich *Spartenbrau* used to be served. Momentarily discouraged by our failure of the night before, we were afraid of having to spend an indefinite period between Aix-la-Chapelle and the spot we had marked out for crossing the frontier. It occurred to us that help from outside would be invaluable ... I had a good friend, almost a brother, on whose affection and intelligence I had always been able to count throughout the fifteen years of our acquaintance – Raoul Humbert. I knew him to be at Leysin (Switzerland) at the sanatorium 'Les Fougères'. I wrote to him. I sent my letter in an envelope of the tavern, where he was to reply to me, using the name of Munder. Disguising my handwriting, I told him that with a fellow-machinist from the firm of Oerlikon, I was held up at Aix-la-Chapelle by an accident to my arm, sustained during a first and unsuccessful attempt to install the motor, that I hoped to have better luck with my second attempt, but that nevertheless I should be glad of his helpful intervention in whatever form he could give it. The terms of my letter were of necessity ambiguous, but my friend Humbert would certainly decipher its meaning without difficulty. I may as well say now that the letter reached him – he has since shown it to me, with the tavern's stamp on it – but on that same day the newspapers announced that Garros and I had reached Holland in safety, and so he did nothing.

Towards evening we went into a sort of café. We were served with *ersatz* coffee, accompanied by a sort of tart, the crust of which was artificial – as indeed were the cream and the strawberries with which it was filled. Our stomachs did not receive it with any better grace than the morning's fourteen mussels.

Night came. Our previous failure would at least have served to teach us the lie of the land, so it was with greater confidence that we started off again towards the frontier. Alas! we went farther astray than ever, only extricating ourselves with the greatest difficulty from the barbed wire and with only the satisfaction of not having attracted the attention of a patrol. Aix had the privilege of seeing our second return between 3 and 4 o'clock.

With no food save that which I have already described this new march of 30 kilometres left us thoroughly exhausted, and we began to fear that we would never succeed in getting out of the damned country. But we had to find a place to sleep in. I led Garros to an inn near the station, where I knocked while my companion waited at a distance. A sleepy woman opened to me. I said that I was called Schmidt, and asked her if a friend of mine, a commercial traveller, had inquired for me that night. She replied in the negative. 'Then he hasn't yet arrived. He will very likely come by a later train, but he will certainly join me before long. In any case, I will take a room for myself and reserve another for him.' My friend, strangely enough, arrived almost immediately. And now for a good sleep. We had earned it.

At midday Garros said: 'Listen, old man. Today is the end. Either we pass the frontier or we are done for. But it isn't after two days and three nights of almost total abstinence that we shall be in the best form for the last pull at the traces. At whatever risk we must have a good feed.'

I agreed with him only too well. In order not to remain for ever at the inn we moved to another hotel in the same quarter. I booked two rooms for the sake of appearances. Then I called the restaurant attendant aside. 'Look here,' I said, 'we have come a long way and are very hungry – only I warn you we have lost our food cards.' He gave me to understand that, if I did not look too closely at the price, the matter might be arranged.

It was arranged. We were served with a dinner, washed down with wine, that would have been perfection save for a total lack of bread. It seemed that everywhere, even in this land of regulations, the severest of restrictive organisations could be circumvented. And that night again, beside the official menu endorsed by the police, we had an enormous steak with potatoes, an omelette and some jam. Nothing was lacking save the bread.

Well ballasted, thoroughly revived, we felt full of courage and spirits. Nevertheless, we redoubled our precautions. Once on our way, we took frequent bearings, in order to make no error in our itinerary, and at the slightest alarm we took refuge behind a bush or in a ditch.

At 7 or 8 kilometres from the frontier the immediate proximity of the principal guard-house was made clearly visible to us by its external illuminations – a huge electric light. In that vicinity the slightest imprudence would be the end of us. We advanced only on hands and knees, ears and eyes well opened. At last we came on a little stream that was noted on our map as marking the last line of sentries. But here we were condemned to a lengthy wait. We were in the first night of the first quarter of the moon, and it shed a considerable amount of light. Until it had set we could not walk, nor even crawl, in the open. We found that it took its time about it. Never had I realised how slowly the moon travels. We cursed it for its sloth. We even accused it of being an hour late according to the meteorological schedule announced for it in the *Magdeburg Journal* that we had consulted. However, neither the moon nor the newspaper was at fault; the error was due to an idiosyncrasy of Garro's watch.

At last the night was dark. We set off again, on all-fours, until we came to a perfectly naked plain. Not a tree, not a house to be seen. No further doubt was possible – we were approaching the goal.

Nevertheless, we were worried by the fact that we could not find the landmark that had been indicated to us – a mountain peak that dominated the otherwise flat country. We could see no slightest trace of the smallest peak, yet we still felt that we were on the right track. This idea was confirmed by the sight, in the distance, of a brilliantly illuminated building, which we had been told to use as a lighthouse. But we had been told that it was the guard-house from which the frontier was watched, whereas in reality it was a coke factory situated in Holland itself. Yet, save for that error of identification, it was the same luminous landmark of which we had been told.

As for the famous mountain peak, which we saw later, it was no more than one of those huge slag-heaps that are so often found in industrial areas.

We advanced now flat on our stomachs, and crossed in that fashion a ploughed field which we saw to be traversed on our right by numerous footprints.

'That must be the route for the relief of the sentries,' we said to ourselves. No matter – we must get on. Crawling thus we made barely 500 metres an hour – and in what state of mind may be imagined – a curious mixture of terror and hope.

Now, 20 metres in front of us, there rose a little thorn hedge. In the breath of a whisper we said to each other that it must border the road along which, if our information was reliable, the sentries patrolled.

At that moment we heard someone cough to our right. Garros seized my arm and pressed it, indicating that we must neither speak nor move. Holding our breath, we did our best to disappear into the ground.

All at once the sentry who had coughed began to walk towards us. Suddenly he stopped. We had the agonising sensation that he could see us perfectly well in the dark. But no, he went on, paused a few metres in front of us, and continued on his way to our left.

He came back, walked to the right, and halted.

Then we heard a voice, to which another replied. It was the conversation of people speaking face to face – nose to nose, judging by the tone of their voices.

Now, we knew that the sentries on that line were posted at intervals of a 150 metres; so if one of them had moved to go and talk to his right-hand neighbour it was highly probable that he had thus opened in front of us a gap double the usual width. We must take advantage of it.

Crawling obliquely towards the left, we reached the thorn hedge. Fortunately there were gaps in it, between the little trunks where they emerged from the soil. By groping, Garros found his and I mine. We slid through.

Beyond it the ground sloped slightly, and a metre and a half farther on a strand of barbed wire was stretched low across the grass.

The wire was arranged in such a manner as to trip up anybody who passed, so that the noise made by his stumbling might warn the sentries. As we were crawling we felt the wire, and did not trip.

We found ourselves now in a little field, about 100 metres wide. Still flat on our stomachs we crossed it. A perfect hedge of barbed wire bounded it. It was the last obstacle. In one bound, taking no heed of torn skin or clothing or rifles or sentries, we leaped on to and over it, and in another we cleared a stream whose sinuous course marked the frontier. Then, with beating hearts, soaring spirits and smarting eyes, we literally fell into each other's arms. We were in Holland! We were out of reach of the Germans.

*　*　*

Here end my souvenirs of captivity. It only remains to me to relate briefly the circumstances of our repatriation.

From the point where we had crossed the last line of German barbed wire we took train for The Hague, where we reported ourselves to the French Ambassador. Garros never forgot, as I shall never forget, the charming manner in which General Boucabeille, the military attaché, the general's wife and the members of the French colony received us.

Then we took ship for England. The crossing was effected in the usual manner, that is to say, under the protection of British destroyers. During the voyage if a mine or two were signalled no fuss was made – our ship and her escort knew well enough how to avoid them. I may note, too, that a German hydroplane attacked us, but its bombs made no victims in our flotilla: the inoffensive fish of the North Sea were the only sufferers.

At last we reached London, and from there we left for Boulogne and the front.

The nightmare was over. We were soldiers once more.

CHAPTER SIX

ESCAPE AT THE FIRST ATTEMPT

By H.G. Durnford

The officers' Lager at Stralsund lay on an island, or rather on a twin pair of islands, called Greater and Smaller Danholm, separated from the mainland by a narrow strip of water over which a permanent ferry plied to and fro. On the farther side of these islands and separated from them again by a wider channel, perhaps two-thirds of the width of the Solent at its narrowest point, lay the pleasant shores of Rügen. The blue sea and the wooded slopes of this fair island recalled to the home sick prisoner the beauties of her smaller sister of the Wight.

Hither in the summer of 1918 came 500-odd hungry British officers, the unwilling guests of his then Imperial Majesty Wilhelm II. They were a not inconsiderable part of the many taken in the three gigantic German offensives between 21st March and 27th May. They came in big batches from the sorting-out camps of Rastatt and Karlsruhe – the former place a memory that will endure for their lives with those who were there – or in little driblets from the hospitals whence they had been discharged. Hither came also in September 200 officers from Aachen (Aix-la-Chapelle), the last of their illusions gone. They had been sent from various camps to that place, the stepping-stone for internment and happier things. They had stayed there two months. Their parcels, which should have been forwarded to them, went persistently 'west'. In many cases even their luggage had gone to Holland. They had been taken for walks and had viewed the promised land. And now, at the eleventh hour, the congestion of sick at Aachen had necessitated their removal and they had been side-tracked to the Baltic-to wait and wait, and begin the dreary round again. They moved our sympathy. They had had two and a half years of it, and now they had as little to eat as, and not much more to wear than, the new arrivals. But one of them had a typewriter.

And hither came also a little party of three from Holzminden Camp in Brunswick, transferred as suspected persons to a camp of really reliable security. Major Gilbert, Lieutenant Ortweiler, and myself had been told one morning that we had an hour and a half in which to pack. We packed and went. Stralsund was like a rest cure.

It is indeed a pleasant spot. A channel, narrow at the entrances, broadening to 90 yards in the middle, divides the islands. Standing on the bridge which spans the channel at its narrowest, one looks west to Stralsund town. Whether with the setting sun behind it or with the morning sun full on it, it is beautiful. Venice viewed from the sea could hardly be prettier. The dome of the Marianne Kirche dominates the town, and the bat-coloured sails of the fishing vessels could be just seen, with an occasional motor-boat, moving in the blue Sound. In Greater Danholm the chestnuts are magnificent. There is one avenue of trees which meet each other overhead as in a cathedral nave. And there was one little segregated, fenced-off spot which for no particular reason we called King Henry VIIIth's Garden – the name seemed to suit. One could take half an hour walking round the camp.

But it is not my intention by painting too glowing a picture to alienate my reader's sympathy. The place was good, but German. The buildings were good, but had held Russians. The air was good, but there were smells. We had been long-time prisoner-veterans, we considered ourselves, in this horde of 'eighteeners'. And it would be cold, very cold in winter.

We had a fortnight's holiday, revelling in the unexpected beauty, the much less uncomfortable beds with their extra sheet, the open-air sea bath in the mornings, the freedom and scope of movement, the almost latent wire, the inoffensiveness of the German personnel, the unobtrusiveness of the Commandant, the beer (liquorice, but still beer of a sort), the exchange of news with the new prisoners and the picking up of old threads, the sight of the sea from our landing window, the games on real grass ...

And then, in quite a different sense, we began looking round.

We learned that the authorities were quietly and politely confident that the place was escape-proof. They expected attempts. Oh! yes. 'We know it is your duty. We should do it ourselves.' And conventionalities of the sort that were common when German officers of a decent type – and there were such on this island – found themselves in conversation with Englishmen. 'But it cannot be done – no one has ever escaped from here. True, it might be easy to cut the wire and get on to the main part of the island, but we have our dogs. If you swim to the mainland you will be recognised and brought back. Even if you get across to Rügen you have to get off it and you would be missed. We have our seaplane to scour the sea. The ferry is guarded...' and so on.

Subsequent events appeared to justify this view. Attempts were made, and failed in quick succession. In each case the objective was the same, though aimed at by different methods – the open sea and the Danish island of Bornholm or Danish territory elsewhere. Two officers, yachtsmen born, cut the wire one night, swam out towards Rügen, boarded an empty fishing vessel about 200 yards out and got clean away. They stranded off the north-west corner of Rügen and were recaptured. Three others commandeered a boat which had been left unpadlocked in the channel, rowed to the mainland, and separated. Two were recaptured immediately, the third was at large some days and was eventually arrested some way down the coast. I did not learn his story. Another party of three attempted to paddle over to Rügen on a cattle trough. They selected a stormy night, were upset 50 yards out of the channel, and got back, unobserved, with difficulty, and, as one of them could not swim, rather luckily.

So far as the German precautions went, the net upshot of these attempts was that stringent orders were issued about leaving boats in the channel or on the shores of the island unpadlocked. For the rest, the Commandant was satisfied with his second line of defence, the water, which was moreover (it was now mid-September) growing daily colder and more unattractive.

Such was the position when the Holzminden trio began to put their heads together. I do not think any of us seriously entertained the idea of an escape by water. We were all hopeless landsmen, and Gilbert, at any rate, could not swim. A 'stunt' by sea necessitated a combination of luck, pluck, opportunism, and above all, watermanship. Our armament, such as it was, was of a different kind. We all knew German, Gilbert and I indifferently, Ortweiler fluently. We had the wherewithal to bribe. We could lay our hands on a typewriter. We knew the ropes of a land journey by railway. G and O had both been 'out', the latter more than once; and I had heard these things much discussed. Moreover, Gilbert, being a Major, had secured a small room which he invited me to share, and Ortweiler was a member of our mess. In a deep-laid scheme privacy is almost an essential. Greatest asset of all, the Germans were not suspicious and they left us alone.

Our idea, very much in the rough, crystallised as follows: together or separately – as events might dictate – to bluff the sentry at the main gate, and at the ferry; to get on to the mainland and there travel by train to the

Holland frontier; and to have our preparations so thoroughly made that, on paper at least, our plan was bound to be successful.

Our first idea was to co-opt three or four others and go out as a party of orderlies with one of us disguised as a German sentry in charge. Individual officers had on several occasions already been into the town with a party of orderlies on some 'fatigue' or other in order to have a look round. Our idea was to concoct some imaginary fatigue which would take us not only into the town but out of it, where we should have an opportunity of assuming our real disguise and separating on our respective routes. We got so far as to fashion out our bogus rifle in the rough, but before very long we discarded the whole idea for various reasons. The rifle would be too difficult to imitate to pass in broad daylight. We could not be certain of securing the uniform of our sentry; all the sentries on duty in the camp were likely to be personally known to one another. Difficulties of taking our disguise with us, difficulties of hitting on the right sort of 'fatigue' to disarm suspicion... the 'cons' had it emphatically.

Moreover, in the interval the looked-for 'key' had presented itself. Gilbert had succeeded in removing a workman's 'permit' from his coat pocket while he was working in the camp. This 'permit' entitled the civilian in question to visit the camp and its environs between given dates, name and business being duly stated, and the permit signed by the Camp Commandant. Printed in German print on a plain white card, it appeared not impossible of exact imitation. Our hopes were more than fulfilled. Lieutenant Lockhead, one of the party weather-bound en route for a neutral country, had, we knew, performed yeoman service in this line when at Holzminden. We showed him the card. Within two days he had accomplished an exact replica, including the signature, so good as to be indistinguishable from the original. Our hopes rose. It remained to complete the remainder of our essential equipment – civilian clothes, German money, forged passports, maps, and compasses. With the two former I was entirely unprovided. One passport, forged on an old model, was in Gilbert's possession, but we doubted its efficacy in northern Germany. The two latter articles I was content to leave to the last moment, when I should have definitely decided on my route. One had the feeling that it was absurd to spend hours on acquiring articles necessary only for the last lap, when one might be stopped at the gate – a curiously illogical reasoning, as these things, or at least one of them, are indispensable for even a short journey across country... but there it was.

It was at this point that the event occurred which led me definitely to abandon my Holland scheme and decide for the Danish border. A German private soldier came into our room one day to do some work. He was in uniform but was on leave in Stralsund, which was his home, and in the then prevailing shortage of labour he was lending a hand to his erstwhile master.

No 'escaper' ever omits a chance – provided he can speak German at all – of profiting by a conversation with someone from outside the camp. Indeed, this was so well known to the authorities that in most camps anybody coming in from outside was escorted by a sentry and not left alone during the period of his stay in the camp. Stralsund was an exception, possibly because the English had been there so short a time, possibly because of the Commandant's complacent idea as to its security. Be that as it may, I had this fellow fairly quickly sized up. It turned out his job was doing sentry on the Denmark border.

'Is it dull there?'

'Frightfully.'

'Do many get over up there?'

'Oh, yes.'

'What? Prisoners?'

'A few, but smugglers and deserters mostly. We pretend not to see them.'

Here was an eye-opener! I threw caution to the winds and found that I had not mistaken my man. He was a genial rascal, venal and disloyal to the core. Before he had been in that room half an hour he had committed himself far too deeply in the eyes of the German law for me to have any fear that he would turn round and blow the gaff on *us*. He told us (Gilbert had come in by that time) of a slackly guarded frontier, with wire so low that you could walk over it; of the exact route from Stralsund to the last station outside the *Grenz-Gebiet* (border territory); of the innocuous passage of an ordinary *Personal-Zug* (slow train) without the complications of passport-checking or examination over the dreaded Kiel Canal. He came in next day with some civilian collars and ties and an inadequate railway map, and on each day he went out the heavier by sundry woollen and flannel clothes, cigarettes, soap, chocolate, and cheese. He gave me in return about 30 marks in German money. He had promised to do even more, but he made some excuse that his leave was up and we saw him no more. Probably he funked it. Viewed as a commercial deal, the balance was in his favour; but he had given us information that was beyond rubies. Our hopes rose higher, and by this time Gilbert and I were more or less definitely committed to the Denmark scheme.

We had not long to wait for an opportunity of seeing how our passports should read. I will say no more. Even at this distance of time, immeasurably magnified by the intervening events, there still may lurk the long arm in German law, and we need not doubt that there are still too many souls in Germany attracted by the thought: *Wie soll ich Detectzive werden?* (How shall I become a detective?) to make it altogether safe for those concerned if I were to be more explicit in print. Suffice it to say that our tools were of tender years, cheaply bought, and therefore on both accounts the less deserving of retribution. I had sold my field service ration boots for 45 marks, through the agency of Ortweiler. I had therefore collected about 75 marks, and this was, of course, ample for my requirements. I was all the time anxiously on the look-out for civilian clothes. I had got a pair of old blue trousers from Captain Clarke of the Merchant Marine. I had an old pair of ration 'Tommy' boots which on comparison with the home-grown article might just 'do'. I had shirt, collar, and tie. I wanted hat, coat, and, in view of the lateness of the season, some sort of overcoat.

By great good luck the hat, or, as it happened, cap materialised. A new naval suit with cap had arrived for a merchant skipper who had gone to Aachen for a medical board with the hope of exchange. As soon as we had heard he had been passed and gone over the border, G and I promptly closed for the suit, of which we had secured the refusal, with his *chargé d'affaires*. Shorn of its buttons the suit made a smart civilian costume for Gilbert, and shorn of its badge the cap became merely of the naval type of headgear so common amongst German boys or men of the working-class. I had always decided I would shape my role according to the clothes which I could find, and I now decided that I should travel fourth class, as some sort of mechanic. For a coat I had to fall back upon a brand new English coat sent out from home and confiscated by and re-stolen from the Germans. I made it as shabby as I could in the short time at my disposal but even so it was far too smart to pass for my class of 'character' except at night. I therefore decided that if travelling by day I would wear over my coat a very old dark blue naval raincoat which had been given me. I was thus equipped. I might possibly have done better if I had waited, but the completion of my arrangements had to synchronise, as far as possible, with that of the others. I had also been able to copy a fairly good map of northern Schleswig, showing roads and railways, and, by great good luck and at the eleventh hour, I secured what I believe was the last compass but one in the whole camp. The shortage of these articles seemed extraordinary, when one reflected on the abundance of them in most of the old camps of longer standing. To the donor on this occasion I am eternally indebted, as I could not have managed very well without it.

From one of the camp personnel I had elucidated the fact that the Hamburg train went at six-forty in the morning. From another source we heard there was also a train at six-forty-three in the evening.

Gilbert meanwhile had been busy with the typewriter which he had secured with great forethought from its owner in the Aachen party. The 'Ausweis' forms were completed, each according to our own particular specifications. Mine ran as follows:

PERSONAL-AUSWEIS

Für

Karl Stein

aus

Stralsund

on the outside, and on the inside: on the left-hand side, my photograph (I had been photographed in this very camp by the Germans and I had been wearing at the time an old Indian volunteer tunic which in the photograph looked much like a German tunic. This was pure chance and very lucky.)

On the right side, my particulars:

Karl Stein.

Date of Birth: *4/6/1880.*
Place of Birth: *Stralsund.*
State belonging to: *Prussian.*   Height: *1.60 metres.*
Chin: *Ordinary.*   Eyes: *Brown.*
Mouth: *Ordinary.*   Hair: *Brown.*
Nose: *Large.*   Beard: *Moustache.*
Particular marks: *None.*
Authentic Signature: *Karl Stein.*
(A very lame and halting hand this!)
'Herewith certified that the owner of the pass has subscribed his name with his own hand.'
(*Signed*) LIEUTENANT OF POLICE, STRALSUND.

The stamps affixed to the passport – two on the photograph, one on the right-hand side – were an amazingly clever imitation by Lockhead (the friend who had already helped us with the forging of the permit cards). He did these stamps by hand through some purple carbon paper that I still had with me from an old army message-form book, and to be believed they should be seen in the original.

G took infinite trouble with the filling up of these passports. He had acquired a good flowing German hand and he filled the particulars in himself, with a flourish for the signature of the Police *Leutnant* at the bottom. He also filled in the permit-cards. We each had two passports, one made out as from Stralsund, and the other as from Schleswig. We should naturally show the Stralsund one in the Schleswig territory and *vice versa*.

We were now ready, or as ready as any one is until the actual time comes, when there are always a thousand and one things to be thought of.

It was arranged amongst ourselves that Ortweiler should have the first shot, as he stood easily the best chance of effecting escape. Accordingly, on Monday, 14 October, he made his exit. He was well made up with a false moustache stuck on with some very diluted form of spirit gum, and fiercely curved at the lips. It was only tow, but it served its purpose in the dark. Our duty was to patrol the avenue leading to the main gate between 5.00 and 6.30pm, to mark down what dangerous Germans had left the camp, and to stop O if anyone who was likely to suspect him hove in sight.

I should mention here that from the barrack selected as dressing-room to the main gate is about 200 yards. From the main gate on to the ferry is another 350 yards. After dark at this time of year various Germans living in the town were likely to be leaving the island for the night, and the ferry was thus constantly on the move. Our object was primarily to avoid the more dangerous Germans, e.g. an officer or the interpreter, who knew us all well by sight.

All went well. I gave the signal 'all clear' at about six-thirty and G and I piloted Ortweiler out, slowing down as he passed us 40 yards from the main gate. We saw him take out his card and hand it to the sentry, who then let him through the postern. It had worked! We breathed a sigh of relief. Just as we were going back, we met the interpreter homeward bound for the ferry. He was too close behind O to be exactly safe, so I engaged him in conversation. He was in a hurry and I could only think of something rather fatuous to say, but I held him up a minute or two and that may have caused him to miss Ortweiler's particular boat.

We 'cooked' Ortweiler's *appel* at 8.00pm – this is a familiar device for concealing escape. The result was that the barrack Feldwebel did not report his absence till next day at 9.00am roll-call. He had thus twelve hours' clear start, by which time he was most of the way to Berlin. We thought him almost a certainty to get over with his fluent knowledge of German, and he did, in point of fact, escape into Holland, *via* Berlin, Frankfort, and Crefeld, after a night's thrilling experience on the actual border which would be a story in itself.

G and I were naturally elated, the more so as from inquiries it transpired that the authorities had absolutely no suspicion of how O had got out. Owing to repeated wire-cutting and escapes into the island, the guard had been increased and placed outside the wire. No one had passed the sentries who had not the proper credentials. Of that they were quite convinced. It was believed that he was still hiding in the camp. We hugged ourselves.

Friday of that week, the 18th, the day selected as '*der Tag*,' was an unforgettable one. Our kit had to be packed and labelled; final arrangements made about feeding in the event of recapture; compromising documents of any sort had to be destroyed; at the last moment I realised that I had no braces, no German cigarettes, and no matches. To crown all there was a barrack hockey match which we could not very well avoid.

During the day it so happened that we were twice invaded by Feldwebels. On the first occasion the door was locked and we had to throw a map into the corner and then open the door, an action which would in itself have been of damning suspicion in most camps. On the second, the Feldwebel found G cutting sandwiches of German *Kriegs Brot* (war bread). G had to explain that it was a new attempt to make *Kriegs Brot* palatable, and invited the Feldwebel to come and see the result at dinner time. Doubtless he came, but there were no sandwiches and no us. At 4.00pm we had our high tea – four Copenhagen eggs each and tea and jam. At 5.00pm the roll was called, and immediately after it we started transferring our disguise under cover of the growing darkness to the barrack from which we were going to make our final exit.

It had been arranged after some discussion that Gilbert should leave not before dark, and not later than six, and that I should give him ten minutes clear before leaving. This would give me little time to catch the six-forty-two train to Hamburg if I was at all held up (a forecast which was verified by events); but there was no help for it. It was necessary that Gilbert's disguise should be assisted to the full by darkness.

We had let a few friends into the secret and these were cruising about like destroyers up and down the avenue, reporting the departure of dangerous Germans, Gilbert did not eventually get off much before six, and it seemed a long time before the leader of the convoy reported that G was safely through the gate. I gave him ten minutes, conscious mainly of the fact that I had forgotten any German I had ever learnt, and then stepped forth.

I was Karl Stein, firm of Karl Stein & Co., Furniture Dealers, Langestrasse, Stralsund; I had been into the Kommandantur to arrange about a new contract for officers' cupboards. I knew the shop because I had seen it the day before when I went to the town hospital under escort with a party of officers for massage. I needed no massage, of course, but had only done this to acquaint myself with the geography of the town.

With a blank stare I passed several brother-officers walking up and down the avenue and reached the gate. My great moment had come, but the sentry simply looked at my card carefully, said *schon*, and handed it back. I walked very fast down to the ferry. There was no boat on my side and I saw I should have to wait some minutes. The sentry at the ferry examined my card and handed it back. How should I avoid the two Germans who were already there on the jetty waiting for the boat? I decided to have a violent fit of coughing.

I must here mention that my knowledge of German, acquired during captivity, was not such as would enable me to support a cross-examination of more than a minute or two. I had, however, practised the 'pure' German accent with assiduity. In point of fact I hardly spoke a hundred words on the journey, and some of these were not absolutely necessary.

At last the ferry boat came over, empty. I got in and sat in the bows. There was an English orderly working the bow oar – I had seen him the previous day. I kicked him, and he realised what I was and shielded me as much as he could from the other occupants of the boat, which was now gradually filling. It was a long five minutes and I continued my violent fit of coughing, leaning over the side as if in a paroxysm. There were two Germans in the bows and one of them touched me on the shoulder and suggested that I should trim the boat by sitting in the middle. I complied meekly, feeling really very wretched indeed.

At the last I thought I was really done for. The German adjutant got into the boat. He didn't know me by sight, but I thought it was more than likely that he would suspect me. Mercifully he began to talk to some lady typists from the camp who had just preceded him.

We shoved off eventually, almost full. I continued coughing till we got across. When the boat discharged I went ashore almost last. I gave them a wide berth in front, and as soon as I was clear made off at my best pace for the station. Now I was Karl Stein of Schleswig, carpenter, ex-army man, and recalled for civilian employment, catching the train for his native country. I tore up my 'permit' and dropped it in the road – one month off my sentence, anyway.

As I expected, I just missed my train. I had no watch, but the clock on the Marianne Kirche showed me I should be late. I reached the station about six-fifty; it was rather full of people. I wondered if Gilbert was away in that train... and then, vaguely, what the chances were of my being nabbed before the next went – this, I noted, was at six-forty the next morning (Saturday). I think if there had been any outgoing trains that night I should have taken them, even though they led me east instead of west. But as it happened there were none. I went into the men's lavatory in the station, shut myself in a closet and reflected. I thought at that time to my horror that I had forgotten my matches, so I denied myself a smoke – my matches turned up later and I needed what few there were. I solaced myself with a slab of chocolate.

The position was not encouraging. Our information about trains was correct. Our friends would not be able to camouflage our absence, which would certainly be discovered by 8.00pm, reported by 9.00pm. It was more than likely that they would telephone to the station. I determined not to be in the station at all between nine and twelve. If I was arrested next morning, I was. In the meantime it was good to be free.

It was a beautiful October night in Stralsund. I braced myself up and begged a light for a cigarette from a youngster at a street corner, and then strolled along the streets that led from the station to the Kirche. I knew these now quite well enough not to get lost. I sat on a bench and looked across the moonlit water, which near the station runs right in in a broad and lovely sweep. I lit a pipe from my German cigarette and smoked comfortably. Should I get off next morning? ...

I was cooling down now, and wandered down past the Marianne Kirche to a cinema in the Langestrasse. A boy there told me the booking office was shut. I wandered round and round till 1 o'clock. I sat for a long time on my old bench overlooking the water; at another place I entered a private garden and sheltered for an hour under a wall right on the water's edge. It was blowing fairly fresh.

About 1 o'clock I returned to the station and entered the waiting-room, full of recumbent figures, mostly soldiers and sailors. I got hold of two chairs and tried to sleep. There was a sailor on the other side of the table.

At 4 o'clock I got up and had a cup of coffee. The waiting room was now fairly full of people, most of them presumably going by my train.

I had by now a two-days' growth of beard and my moustache was fairly long and well down over the corners of my mouth. Moreover, I had had a fairly sleepless night.

In my pockets I carried three large sandwiches of German bread with English potted meat inside, about twenty slabs of Caley's marching chocolate, a box of Horlick's milk tablets, a spare pair of socks, some rag and vaseline, my pipe and tobacco, English and German cigarettes, my compass, money, and papers. I had an old German novel in my hands which I pretended to read with great assiduity. Half an hour before the train was due to start, I went to the booking office. I was surprised to hear my own voice. 'Fourth to Hamburg, please.' I had no idea what it cost, so I tendered a 20-mark note. The ticket cost only 7 marks! I went back to the waiting-room, and a few minutes later faced the barrier. No questions, no suspicion. I breathed again and wondered what that Commandant had done. Wired to Rostock perhaps ...

My carriage was not over-full at the start – four or five women and two elderly men. I had no trouble with them. Their conversation began and maintained itself exclusively about food, but they were cheerful enough.

Before Rostock the carriage had filled up and I with British politeness was strap-hanging. An old woman began asking me to shift her *Korb* (basket). I could not exactly understand what she wanted and must have looked rather foolish. However, I did the right thing eventually.

We changed at Rostock. I was half-expecting trouble but nothing happened. A porter told me the platform for the Hamburg train. I got this stereotyped question fairly pat.

To Hamburg the train was overflowing; we were over forty in a tiny compartment. I was wedged in against the window, strap-hanging. At one intermediate station a young soldier got in with a goose hanging out of his haversack. He immediately became the centre of an admiring throng. He was a cheerful youth and bandied repartee with all and sundry – I could not catch his sallies, which were in low German and greeted with roars of laughter. I suppose he was the son of some farmer and had 'wangled' this goose, which would probably have fetched 150 marks in the market, to take back to his messmates. He got out just before Hamburg. I could not have asked for a better foil.

Hamburg! I had never hoped for even so long a run as this. Was there really a chance? . . . In any case, I was now well clear of the Stralsund zone. I began to realise that the heavy weekend traffic was helping me and that I was indeed no more than a needle in a haystack. I ate a sandwich and an apple which I had bought at Lubeck.

We ran into the big station at about two-forty in the afternoon – it was very full. It did not take me long to find the 'departure' notices, Kiel three-ten. I took my place in the 'queue' for the fourth-class booking office. Behind me two women had an altercation as to priority of place in the 'queue'. I was rather afraid they were going to appeal to me. I had no wish for the role of Solomon at that moment.

I booked direct to Flensburg –about 4 marks' worth – and made my way downstairs to the departure platform, which was indicated clearly enough. I did not like the odd quarter of an hour which I had to wait before the train came in. I was not very happy about my dark-blue water-proof. I could not see anything approaching its counterpart. If one stands still, one can be examined at leisure; if one moves up and down, one runs the gauntlet of a hundred restless eyes, any one pair of which may at some previous date have had first-hand cognisance of a typical naval rubber-lined English waterproof . . .

Then I blundered. There was a coffee-stall on the platform. I went up to it and asked for a cup. I had drunk nothing since 4 o'clock in the morning. Fortunately neither of the *Frauleins* in the stall paid any attention to me. Just then I saw the notice '*for soldiers and sailors only*' printed up in big letters. I should have known that, but no one had noticed anything.

When *would* that train come in?

It came at last. I chose the carriage with fewest soldiers in it, and most women, and made for my strategical position by the window. But it was impossible to avoid men altogether. I had one strap hanging next to me from Hamburg to Kiel. Everybody started chattering at once. How could I keep out of this all the way to Kiel without suspicion? Of course, they were talking about food – various ways of dishing up potatoes.

I looked out of the window, pretending to be interested in the country. It was impossible even to pretend to read in that crush. A man on the seat was forcibly expressing his views to two *Frauleins* on the new (10th) War Loan. They giggled.

I often wonder if those Hamburg folk then had any notion that another fortnight would see the Red Flag floating in their midst.

At Neumünster we had an invasion. The carriage, full already, became packed. Four girls of the farmer class – sisters, I judged them – got in at my window. I lost my place of vantage and was relegated to the middle of the floor. I felt a pasty-faced youth quite close to me sizing me up …

Fortunately the farmer girls riveted all attention for half a dozen stations. They were in boisterous spirits and screamed with laughter at their own jokes. They spoke dialect and I could not understand them, but I grinned feebly in unison. When they got out, I recovered my post by the window. Bless them, anyway, for a diversion.

At the next station an elderly man who was sitting on a basket immediately in front of me said something to me directly. He was not in any way a formidable character, but he spoke villainous dialect and I could not make head or tail of his question. He was referring to something in the station. I said *Ja* and looked out of the window in a knowing way. But I could not risk a second question. I felt the pasty-faced youth's eyes on me again, and I made a bee-line for the lavatory. When I emerged I took up a fresh position.

The train was emptying as we approached Kiel, and for a time I got my head out of the window and enjoyed the draught. Then a little girl standing by me asked me to pull up the window again. I had my second sandwich.

We ran into Kiel at about 6 o'clock. There was no difficulty. A guard, in answer to my question, pointed at the Flensburg train. The carriage I got into was not lit at all and almost empty. What a relief to sit! A girl came in to check my ticket, and I went to sleep. We went over the canal in the dark. There were two men in my carriage. I woke up at some wayside station and asked if it was Flensburg. They laughed and said Flensburg was two hours away yet. I muttered sleepily that I was a stranger, and pretended to drop off again.

I reached Flensburg about 10.30pm, and thought of the unforgettable scene in *The Riddle of the Sands*. I was no less depressed than Carruthers on that occasion. I was very thirsty, but it was a poky little station and there was nothing in the shape of a waiting-room or coffee-stall. I lingered on the platform and saw a porter who appeared to be closing down for the night. I asked him what time the train to Tondern went next day. He first said 6 o'clock, but then reflected that the next day was Sunday and there would not be a train till eleven. He added that the train went from the other station. So there were two stations in Flensburg! My sentry friend had not told me this. I asked him where the other station was and he directed me. My German at this juncture was so abominable that I think he must have been a Dane.

At the other station, which I found to be the main one, there was a fairly large crowd in the booking hall. They were waiting for the incoming 11 o'clock train from the north. Entry to the platform and waiting-rooms was barred. The train came in, the crowd dissolved, and the station was shut up for the night. I had got to put in twelve dreary hours in this place.

I took risks that night in Flensburg, risks that might have been fatal farther south. I argued that here if anywhere one might expect to find a scrubby-faced man with a nautical cap and overcoat. I walked for about an hour past the quays, past the two main hotels, then up towards the church and down again to the quays. I could find no public drinking fountain, which was what I was looking for, but I had learned the rough geography of the place.

There was a low barrier leading on to one of the quays. The gate was locked but I climbed the barrier and sat down on a bench. Behind me was one of those pavilions such as are seen on an English pier-head; in front, a steamer moored alongside. Both were quite deserted. Here at least I could sit and find solitude.

I took off my boots and attended to one of my toes which I had rubbed playing hockey the day before – what weeks ago it seemed! I went through my pockets and – joy! – found my matches. I smoked a luxurious pipe. Then, still in my socks, I boarded the steamer and searched her for water without success. She was fitted up for passengers and for a moment I entertained the idea of stowing myself away on her.

Just as I had finished putting on my boots again a man – a night watch-man I suppose he was – came on to the quay from the left. He must have been attracted by some movement. I confess I thought it was all up.

'What are you doing here?'

'Nothing.'

'But you have no business to be here at all.'

Silence implied assent. He beckoned me after him. He was not a Prussian, this man, whatever else he was. Perhaps he was afraid of me. He appeared to be taking me into some form of building on my right. I pretended to be coming along after him, when I swerved to the right, scrambled over the barrier and ran for 200 yards down the street. Fortunately there was no one about. I was not followed. I was thankful I had got my boots on in time.

I passed the first hotel and saw a woman with a man carrying her bag go in and ask for a room. She got one. I followed in after her and asked for a bed. The proprietor said he was full up and shut the door in my face. Could a two days' growth of beard make such a difference in a man? I was rather hurt.

But worse was to follow. I entered another hotel and saw some German sailors being given the keys of their bedrooms by a Fraulein. I asked her for some coffee. 'No.'

'Water?'

'No.'

'Nothing to drink?'

'No, nothing.'

I came to my senses and fled ...

I went up towards the church, which stands on the top of a steep hill. There are some gardens sloping down the hill. I found an old sort of summer-house in one of these and went to sleep. It was about 1.00am, and none too warm.

I was up at dawn and started again on my weary pilgrimage of the streets of Flensburg. How I hated that place! I half-thought of altering my plan and doing the rest of the journey on foot. It was about 70 kilometres to the frontier.

I passed three military policemen in half an hour and wondered resentfully what they were doing in such large quantities on a *Sunday* morning.

At about eight I got to the station, and ate my last sandwich. Assuming that the porter had been right the previous night, I had got to put in three hours more dreary waiting. There was no overhead notices, but I noticed a useful-looking collection of time-tables stuck up on big boards in a little alcove just out of the booking hall. If I could get behind the rearmost of these I could put in much of my time unobserved. People might come and people might go, but they would never dream that I had been there all the time.

I examined the time-tables. I could make nothing of the Sunday trains, but I found the name Ober-Jersthal. That had been the station given by our informant at Stralsund as the last station outside the *Grenz-Gebiet*. In the maps we had seen in the camp we had never been able to verify this place. Ober-Jersthal must be on the main line running up the east Schleswig coast. So far so good, but at what time would this train go? It could not be the same train as the Tondern train, for Tondern is west Schleswig.

I wandered on to the platform. The bookstall was open and I bought a paper and also a Pocket Railway Guide. The Guide had a good map. I saw from this that the Tondern and Ober-Jersthal lines branched off at Tingleff – possibly the two trains went in one as far as Tingleff.

I had not long to wait for corroboration. At the cloak-room I heard a man ask the attendant what time the train went for a station which I knew to be north of Ober-Jersthal on the same line. The answer was eleven-three. There could be no doubt of it now. I booked for Ober-Jersthal. I had still an hour to wait. It passed somehow. I went into the waiting-room and got my first drink for twenty-nine hours, a glass of beer; it was washy stuff but went down wonderfully well. There was a lot of *Matrosen* (sailors) in the waiting-room. Some of them stared at me and I began to have the Hamburg platform haunted sensation over again. I pretended to read my paper fiercely for half an hour and then went on to the platform. I began to regret that I had not had a shave that morning.

The train came in punctually. There was no incident till Tingleff, about 20 kilometres northward. There I saw the passport officials waiting on the platform. I had almost forgotten about this part of the business ...

I took a sudden resolution and left the train. I reckoned that I had not more than 40 miles to walk from this point, and by alighting here I might dodge the passport men altogether. But I was undeceived. An official was waiting at the entrance to the subway. He looked an easy-going fellow and was engaged in conversation with someone. He took my passport, glanced at it, and handed it back without a word. He did not even look to compare my face with the photograph. The great moment which Gilbert and I had rehearsed countless times had come and gone.

I hurried through the subway, and saw another passport official talking to the ticket collector. I handed in my Ober-Jersthal ticket. The man looked up in some surprise, but I was ready for him.

'I have shortened my journey.'

'*Ach! So.*'

He asked no more questions. If he had, I doubt if I could have answered them. I was conscious only of one great wish, to be rid of the railway for good. I struck due north out of the station and found myself in a *cul-de-sac*. I was so overjoyed to be quit of the rail that I plunged into the fields. I had not gone very far before I had reason to repent. There was water everywhere, and I made very heavy weather of it. My objective was Lügumkloster, about 20 miles north-west from Tingleff, and I reckoned that it could not be very long before I struck the main road. After about two hours – it was now 2 o'clock in the afternoon – I found the road. There were very few people about, and those I met gave me good day civilly enough. If questioned at this point, I was going to have been a South German staying with relatives in Flensburg and out for a cross-country ramble – an improbable enough story.

My hopes had risen and it all seemed reasonably plain sailing now. The people were not suspicious. I had my map with a few important names... my compass... I might even do it in the next night.

I wondered exactly where old Gilbert was at this moment. It never even occurred to me that he had been caught, but such, as afterwards transpired, must have been the case.

Passing through one village I met some French prisoners. I gave them good-day and told them who I was. They invited me to come into their room in the farm where they were working. They were able to tell me what village I was in, Dollderup, and this was a great assistance. I thanked them in execrable French, gave them one of my remaining cigarettes, and told them what news I could – they had heard nothing for months. I don't think anything on the whole journey was more difficult than framing those few simple French sentences.

The signposts made the journey easy after that. At 3.00pm I had 18 kilometres to go to Lügumkloster. I turned off the road, lay down in some young fir trees, took off my boots, ate some chocolate, and had half an hour or more's sleep.

I started again towards dusk. I was feeling very fit now and full of hope. If only I didn't muck it on the frontier ... The signposts did their duty nobly. There was a keen wind from the north and the road was good. I had been out just two complete days.

In one village a soldier with a rifle came out of a house just as I passed it. He replied to my '*Guten Abend*' courteously.

I reached Lügumkloster, I suppose, about half-past nine or ten. It is a big rambling village, and I made a bad mistake here on leaving it. I meant to take the Arrip-Amum road, which runs roughly north-east. I took a road running north-east, but after about an hour's walking I found it was leading me gradually more east than north – I had not noticed that the wind had shifted from north to east. I decided to leave the road and make due north on the compass, trusting to pick up the right road later on. Then began a trying time. The ground was terribly wet and intersected with continual wired ditches. I tore my clothes rather badly here and I don't think my trousers at the end of my journey would have stood another rip. However, I kept due north, tacking as little as possible to avoid the ditches, and eventually reached the road. It was, I supposed, about 2.00am I estimated I was still quite 10 miles from the frontier. There was a strong wind, and I had not enough matches to spare to look more than once or twice at my map. Added to this, the signposts, previously so well-behaved, became infuriating. They only mentioned names which I had nover (*sic.*) heard of, or at least had not committed to memory.

Slog! Slog! Slog! I was getting tired. A man passed me with a cart. What on earth did *he* think he was doing at that time of night? There was lots of water about and I did not go thirsty. My cap made an effective cup.

A light railway running parallel to the road – this was the *Klein Bahn* (light railway) the fellow had told us of.

Slog! Slog! Sl. . . – What on earth was that? A sentry box on the roadside, and in the box a sentry yawning and stretching himself. On each side of the road a belt of barbed wire running east and west.

I took these things in vaguely, disconnectedly. Had I miscalculated and was I over the border after all? He hadn't even challenged . . .

A mile later I crawled into a little hollow by the roadside to rest and get warm. I was getting strangely light-headed. I remember addressing myself as a separate entity. I pulled myself together and sat down to think. 'I must go back and have another look at that wire. It can only be a protective belt for military purposes.'

I went back. The wire was there sure enough. So was the sentry box, but I didn't go up to it. The wire was like the rear defence lines one had seen in France.

I retraced my steps. I still had the idea of picking myself up from the hollow where I had left myself.

I continued my way, praying for the night to end. With the dawn, I felt I should be able to think clearly again.

'Arnum 4 kilometres.' The signposts were German enough, anyway.

Arnum, I had made out from my map, lay about 3 or 4 kilometres away from the point of the salient where I meant to cross the border. It was nearly dawn and I saw that I could not get over that night.

It was getting light as I reached the village. I left the road and struck west across the fields, up on to some high ground.

Somewhere in front there was Denmark. I chose a hiding-place in some young firs and heather. I was sheltered from the wind and was fairly comfortable.

One more whole day! What an age it seemed! I got out my railway map and looked at my position. I could not be more than 5 or 6 kilometres from the frontier. Somewhere in the valley to the north-west stretched the line of sentries. I decided to sally forth while it was still light in the late afternoon, take my bearings, and go over at dark.

As I lay there I heard footsteps. A boy came by singing and passed within 2 yards of me. He didn't see me. Just as well perhaps ...

I took off my boots, rubbed my feet down, and had some chocolate.

About noon it started raining and went on for about three hours. I got wet through, but welcomed the rain on the whole as it would get darker sooner.

I was now thinking quite connectedly, and, it being impossible to sleep, I went over in my mind again and again what I meant to do, and what I knew already about the frontier.

I suppose it was about five when I started out. I reckoned there would be about one more hour's daylight. I steered due north-west across fields and marsh land for about 3 kilometres. Suddenly, to my right – about 400 yards off – the sentries' boxes came full in view. There was no mistaking them, about 200 yards between most of them, and quite 300 yards between the two opposite me.

I plumped down in the heather and watched them. I saw a sentry leave his box and walk about 20 yards up and down. I could see nothing that looked like wire. Only marsh and heather in between ...

Looking from where I was into Denmark, there was a farmhouse immediately between the two sentry boxes. I could take my course on that – it would be silhouetted long after dark.

I waited till it was quite dark, and then started off, taking no risks – crawling. I came to a ditch with wire on each side of it. This was the only wire I saw. When I judged I was well through the line, I got up and walked to the farmhouse. A tall figure answered my knock. I began in my best German...

He shook his head to indicate that he didn't understand. I could have kissed him. At last we hammered it out.

'*Engelsk Offizier. Fangen. Gut.*'

He beckoned me in with beaming face.

I had made good in just seventy-two hours. Beginners' luck!

CHAPTER SEVEN

A JOURNEY TO BRUSSELS

By Marthe McKenna

Summer had come. The sun shone down brilliantly on life in Roulers, and the songs of the birds made a pleasant contrast to the almost incessant roll of gun-fire. Stray shells still soared over the town occasionally, but they usually exploded in the air or plunged harmlessly into the fields. Curiously enough, for all that year the casualties from shell-fire had only been two aged cart-horses, which were to be sent to the knacker's yard within a few days in any case!

It suddenly began to strike me that something unusual was happening in Roulers. There was a tremendous air of animation among the Germans, but their activity was of a new kind, and not like that which used to take place before an attack. Sometimes it looked as though our conquerors had all gone mad. Fatigue parties spent their days polishing the floors of the hospital till they glimmered like glass, and men were tying rags on the end of long poles in order to dust the lofty ceilings. In the streets the German soldiers walked in clean new uniforms, and their equipment seemed to have lost its battered appearance. Squads paraded in the streets, moving like automatons, practising the goose-step with eyes and faces of wood. Alphonse grumbled to me that he had had to spend the whole of the last evening, after returning from a heavy day with the ambulance under fire, in polishing and burnishing an aluminium bath in his barrack-room, and that when he had proudly displayed it glistening like a mirror to the hospital sergeant-major, he had condemned it as terrible, and called him an idler. He said that the troops in all the billets throughout Roulers were being put to work in the same way, and that everywhere the officers were making themselves unpleasant to the NCOs, and that consequently these were working off their resentment twofold on the men. He told me that one old soldier, who had been a conscript before the War, said grimly that things were beginning to get quite like the good old times again!

I asked one of the doctors in the hospital what all the excitement was about. He said nobody knew, but that HQ had suddenly decided for some

reason to hurl the full force of its frightfulness upon the Roulers authorities, and that we were all feeling the concussion. I knew there must be
some reason for this. Then one day Alphonse met me in the corridor. He
paused for a moment in passing and said in an undertone:

'The Kaiser is due at Menin next week. He will be coming on here later.
Can you find out the date and time?'

So that was it. I might have guessed. All that day I racked my brains how
to get reliable information. Suppose that I succeeded in bringing about
the death of the German Emperor. It was said that it was he who was
responsible for the War; what, therefore, would happen at his death?
A sharp thrill of excitement ran through me, and I determined that there
must be no mistake in this affair. Yet who in Roulers could provide me
with the necessary information? It was well known that the Kaiser always
kept his movements as secret as possible for fear of attempts on his life.
The Monday of the week before the Kaiser's expected visit came, but my
head was empty of ideas, and I began to despair.

'Canteen Ma' called at the door early. As she handed me our weekly
vegetables, and I was examining them for freshness, she slipped a pincushion into my hand. So they also knew! When I ripped open the
pincushion in my room the message read: 'Kaiser arrives Roulers latter
half next week for brief inspection. Time and Date, etc., for information
British aircraft.'

Elegant staff officers with tight waists and important faces began to
flood Roulers. Then generals arrived in cars, and everybody went about
in a bad temper. The General Staff arrived in person to see that everything in Roulers was lit for the eyes of the mighty war-lord, and the heel-
clicking could have been heard in Ypres.

When I answered a summons to the Oberartz' office on the Tuesday
morning in the week before the expected Royal visit, he was seated with
a tall Staff-Colonel, one of these steely-blue-eyed men with fierce fair
moustaches brushed upwards. He rose smartly upon being introduced,
bowed, clicked his heels, smiled in a refined manner, and bowed again.
The Oberartz asked me to show the Colonel round the wards and to
explain everything to him, excusing himself on the count that a number of
bad cases had just been brought in and that his presence was needed in the
operating theatre.

The Colonel followed me round, always seeming interested, always
courteous. He never found fault with anything, and from time to time
uttered well-bred little jokes to me which evidently amused him tremen-
dously and which I pretended to be much amused at myself. He was

certainly a very polished person. As we approached the door of the Oberartz' office on our return, he surprised me by suddenly saying:

'Perhaps if you find yourself free you would care to lunch with me tomorrow, mein Fräulein?' The Colonel had shown himself to be a talkative man, and I saw a glimmer of hope in this direction. 'There is nothing would please me better, Herr Colonel,' I assured him.

It might be said of that lunch next day that we got along 'famously'. At the end he swallowed his liqueur and called for a second.

'Mein Fräulein,' he smiled, 'life must be tedious in the extreme here in Roulers for a girl of your standing and education.' He gestured with his cigarette gracefully. Would you not come for a while to Brussels, to see the opera, to eat decent food?' I coloured. Food was not what he was thinking about. His hand clasped my wrist.

'Do not be afraid, little one,' he soothed. 'It shall be as you wish. I shall not urge you. Come – and I will strive my utmost to make your stay a pleasure. I will personally guarantee your safety, and I can procure for you a special pass. And now I will escort you to the hospital, Fräulein. As for what I suggest, it is for you to decide.' He rose and pulled back my chair.

Near the hospital gates the road was deserted and he paused and caught my arm. Then gently raising my chin so that his blue eyes gazed into mine he murmured: 'Well, have you decided, mein Fräulein?' I had been thinking furiously during the walk to the hospital.

'Herr Colonel,' I said, 'I have decided. I will stay with you in Brussels.' He kissed my hand gently.

'What excuse will you make to obtain leave of absence from the hospital?' he asked, a trifle anxiously.

'My grandmother lives in Brussels. I will tell the Herr Oberartz that she is very ill and is asking to see me, and that you, Herr Colonel, have had the goodness to procure for me a pass.'

'That is so,' he laughed, 'I am a good Samaritan, indeed!' His arm was about my shoulder, and I think he would have kissed me had not a couple of young officers turned into the street and saluted him rigidly as they passed. 'Take the evening train tomorrow,' he went on, his eyes returning to mine. 'You should be at Brussels soon after midnight. It is possible I may have night work, I do not know. At all events my orderly shall meet you and bring you to my hotel, where a room shall be ready for you. I shall hope for the honour of your presence at breakfast at eight-thirty the following morning.'

'I shall not be able to obtain leave for more than four days from the Oberartz,' I told him; for I had rapidly calculated that that was the longest I could afford to find out the information I wanted, if I was to return to

Roulers and transmit what I knew over the frontier. I might hear nothing, but on the other hand, this man was on the General Staff, and I might well trick him into speaking in an unguarded moment.

The Colonel saluted. 'Mein Fräulein,' he said softly, 'it will be four days of Paradise. Until eight-thirty Friday, and the pass shall reach you tomorrow morning.' He bent sharply from the waist, straightened, turned about and swaggered gaily up the dusty road. I stood watching his receding back, and the scent of the clusters of heliotrope on a nearby wall came to me on the warm air. It all seemed unreal and dreamlike. Had I really promised this stranger that I would spend four days with him in Brussels? Was I mad? To what had I committed myself? What chance had I of coming through such an escapade unscathed? Why had I done it? For the sake of ravished Belgium. The thought comforted me, and I hurried through the grey stone gates and busied myself with other things.

On the Thursday morning before I left for the hospital a German soldier brought an official envelope to the café. It held the special pass and a travelling voucher. I said nothing to my mother of where I was going, for although she encouraged me in spying, I was afraid to tell her of the extreme risk to which I had now committed myself. I did warn her, however, that that night I had a long errand to perform which might keep me away for several days, but there was no cause for unusual anxiety. Now that my course was set, I felt no qualms. If I succeeded no sacrifice could be too great. I left a note for 'Canteen Ma', giving her all details, and requesting as an afterthought that some other secret agent might be near me in the hotel in case of trouble, or in case I was myself unable to transmit information I was able to obtain. I suggested that an agent might pick me up at my hotel in Brussels, by reason of the fact that always, when not in evening dress, I would wear a button-hole of mixed snowdrops and violets without any green leaves at my collar.

A German military car was waiting outside the darkened station at Brussels, and the driver had soon settled me comfortably inside with my single suitcase. He handed me a note from the Colonel, excusing himself for his enforced absence and assuring me that for the future he had made arrangements that he should not be so detained.

I awoke next morning to find a trim maid letting up the blinds and flooding my spacious, unfamiliar bedroom with dazzling sunbeams. The silken curtains, the rich pile carpets, the wallpaper, and the soft billowing eiderdown were of deep peacock blue, and the dark furniture and the electric stove gleamed brightly. Upon the tray on which was my morning coffee was a small note in the Colonel's handwriting, and I did not need to open it to find a dead weight clutching at my heart. It had brought me back to realities. Within the hour I must meet my Colonel, and then what would follow? But somewhere near here was the Kaiser! How I hated this man whom I had never seen. This man whose vandals had overrun my country. I must keep a clear head no matter what should happen. And, ruminating thus, I dressed.

My Colonel was delighted when I appeared in the spacious dining-room, and he devoured a huge breakfast with a light heart and much excited chatter. Being Belgian, and quite unused to a heavy meal and so much good-humour at this early hour, I left somewhat overwhelmed. After I had seen him off with promises to meet at lunch, I determined on a visit to the shops.

Walking along the Rue Royale towards the Grand Place it was heart-rending to see the change in beautiful 'Petite Paris.' Captured Allied guns stood in every possible space, some placarded with inspired news. The roadways badly needed repairs. It all looked shabby in the extreme. The thought struck me that I would like to let loose an army of mad painters to work their will, no matter what the result, so long as that drab, seedy look was eliminated. It suddenly struck me, too, that, irony of ironies! It was 21 July! – Belgium's Independence Day, and here were a horde of marauders in field-green lording it in Beautiful Brussels. The passers-by did not seem cowed by any manner of means. Thank God, every one wore a stiff upper lip.

The shops were a great disappointment. 'It is regrettable, Mademoiselle, but we are unable to renew anything. Our stock is being gradually decreased, and where we are going to get fresh stock from, only the good Lord can say.' The prices asked took my breath away. The half-blue painted shop-windows wore a thin look, for dummy show was everywhere. I nearly wept. I thought I would take a look at the old Grand Place. It was a spot that had always a restful appeal to me. Its noble and towering architecture would drive away my fit of blues.

Turning into the Boulevard Anspach I saw, trudging along, a company of English soldiers. Their prisoners' uniforms were dreadfully shabby, patches everywhere, and with pitiful, down-at-heel boots. The company drew along the kerb as a tramway car clanged its way down the street. As the car drew level with the prisoners a shower of cigarettes and tablets of chocolates fell amongst them from the windows. One of the German guards caught sight of the person on the tramcar who had thrown the edibles. With a loud shout he mounted the moving tram to arrest the culprit who had dared to violate a strict order. The civilian, seeing that he was discovered, vaulted lightly over the iron gate of the tramcar and made rapidly for a side-street off the Boulevard Anspach, the soldier following in hot pursuit, his rifle held at the ready. As the soldier arrived at the opposite footpath, he was obstructed by a small crowd of civilians who in their haste to get out of his way encumbered him the more. Suddenly I saw a foot slyly pushed forward, and the soldier lay sprawled and cursing on the footpath. The foot belonged to the mysterious safety-pin man whom I had last seen that night in the café, when he had stabbed the military policeman and effected the double escape. He faded into the crowd.

The Colonel had returned, and we had just sat down to lunch when I was aware of the noise of distant cheers, which gradually swelled closer, till I could distinguish that they came from Belgian throats; the tramcars passing the hotel seemed to clang their bells with a louder, more insistent warning, and the commotion outside grew in volume. Springing to our feet we hurried into the entrance lobby. The door was packed with the guests, all straining their necks upwards. I gradually pushed my way through, and there a sight met my eyes which thrilled me through and through. An enormous toy balloon was floating free and unfettered, 250 feet above us. It was bedecked in Belgium's national colours, the envelope painted with the Tricolour of France and Union Jack of Britain. Long streamers flew proudly from the sides, 'Vive la Belgique,' 'Vive les Alliés,' embossed thereon. It sailed majestically along in the faint July breeze. A defiant gesture, and a reminder to the invader that Belgium was still in soul free and independent. It was amazing to see the electrical effect on the civilians. Laughing jokes and words of encouragement were passed to each other as they went by, heads held more erect. The Belgian tramcar drivers beat a methodical and persistent tattoo on the tram-bells, motor-drivers gave answering toots, the cabbies cracked their whips defiantly. Deafening noises of all descriptions rent the air until a muttering roar rose over the whole city as the emblem of freedom slowly swept away. I heard the sharp crack, crack of rifles. The military authorities had given orders for the offending emblem to be destroyed. At each crack the tumult swelled the louder, until a final crack and the envelope was no more. The muttering grew fainter and fainter, but Brussels had celebrated its Independence Day!

The Colonel was furious over the affair. 'Himmel,' he said, 'the organisers of such an outrage, a few irresponsible youths I suppose, little think what the result of such a stupid escapade can mean for the town.'

'After all,' I reminded him innocently, 'we have to celebrate our Independence Day some way or another. And then our Independence is only eighty-five years of age! – Youth will have its fling, you know.'

In the evening my gallant entertainer conducted me to a motor car. No orders were given, the driver evidently knew his destination. During our short journey I noticed that all the street-lamps and tramcar lights were painted a dark blue. The sky was slashed by the long beams of questing searchlights, and the distant staccato of anti-aircraft guns told of the activity of Allied raiders. The car pulled up at the entrance to an imposing private residence, set in its own grounds amid trees and shrubs. Several motor cars were parked in the grounds. A ring at the doorbell, a muttered conversation, and we were allowed to enter.

Strains of soft dance music greeted us as I let the attendant take my cloak. We descended marble steps into a beautifully appointed room, profusely decked with flowers and fragrant with perfume. Along one side of the room were red-curtained alcoves, and windows opened on to a shadowy lane along the other side. Ranged round a small dance-floor in the centre were tables. At these tables I saw noisy parties of officers of all services, and with them sat many beautiful girls with tired eyes, some Belgian, some German. Most of them were voluptuously wanton in their behaviour, for the champagne was flowing freely.

A bowing waiter led us to an alcove, and champagne was served to us. The hidden orchestra broke into a lively dance-tune. Almost without exception the officers wore that German class mark, a horrid gash down the side of the face received in some fencing brawl. Some wore monocles, and all had closely cropped hair. And the women – but who am I to judge, for my own country-women were there too! If asked, every one of them would have a harrowing tale to tell. Hounded down, driven to distraction by punishments meted out to their kinsfolk, subject to atrocities and unmentionable acts of outrage, they were caught in a holocaust over which they had no control, until they were literally driven into the arms of their oppressors by sheer want and starvation, utterly bewildered by a world gone mad. In all conscience the blame lay at the door of the invaders. The place was an ultra-select night rendezvous, a product and importation of warring Germany.

As the night passed into morning the company became madly uproarious, singing in uncertain chorus, shouting and embracing. Three noisy late-comers, very drunk, were going the rounds of the centre tables. One of them, a Lutheran minister, carrying a huge stock-whip, beat a drunken tattoo on each table with the whip, until, at one table, unable to keep his balance, he swept off several glasses which fell to the ground with a shattering noise. Wine stained one of the girl's dresses. She struck the minister savagely in the face. He raised his whip, calling her 'A filthy

Belgian sow.' The other officers at the table grew excited. He was pushed away and fell crashing on to another table with a roar of rage.

The scene might have developed into a very nasty episode, for I saw the Colonel's face grow set, but for a stern interruption from the entrance: 'Gentlemen,' grated a harsh voice, 'by orders of the General Commanding, all officers must report to units at once. All civilians not of German nationality must produce their identity cards for my inspection.'

Faint screams of protest came from the frightened girls, who hurried out of the room to seek for identity cards. The Colonel gripped my arm and whispered: 'Say nothing. I will arrange this with the field-major. Von Bissing has lost no time. His chastisement of the town for the balloon imprudence comes quickly.'

When we reached the hotel we heard that Brussels was to be fined 8,000,000 marks, and that curfew was to be curtailed to 5 o'clock until further notice.

Three days passed at the hotel while the Colonel entertained me in the intervals of arduous duty. Had he not been an enemy officer he would have seemed a very pleasant companion. He was courteous, and honestly tried to do all he could to please me. I knew that I greatly attracted him, but beyond caressing my arm or my hand, and presenting me with flowers and small presents, he had paid me none of the attentions I had expected from his manner in Roulers.

Nor had he once visited my room.

Then on the next morning I returned to my room in the hotel after I had been shopping, to see the door standing half-open. At first I thought it was the servant who was late in cleaning out the room, but when I pushed the door wide, a German soldier was standing with his back to me gazing out of the open window. He had just placed two strange suitcases on the ground beside the bed. Then he touched his military cap, and smirking faintly walked out without a word. I knew what this meant. There could be no mistake in the rooms, for the Colonel's initials were on the suitcases. I sat down upon the edge of the bed, aghast. In my silly optimism I had begun to think I might learn what I wanted without having to go to such an extreme. I felt horribly lonely and frightened in a world of savage ogres as I dug my fingers miserably into the silk eider-down, and the tears swelled to my eyes.

But this was absurd. Anything which had come to pass I had brought upon myself. I was a Secret Service agent, not a ridiculous young girl. I looked at my wrist watch, and it was about the hour when the Colonel returned to the hotel from his morning's work. He would probably be waiting for me over his vermouth in the lounge at this moment. Perhaps, smiling to himself at the trick he had played me. But was it a trick? Could I have expected anything else? I left the bed, powdered my nose, tidied my hair, and slowly proceeded downstairs, wondering how the Colonel would greet me.

In the lounge the Colonel left the palm-shaded alcove where he had been sitting and approached me with his well-bred smile. Bowing, he kissed my hand and conducted me back to his alcove, after ordering further drinks. He was suave and his talk was of trivialities. He made not the slightest hint about the suitcases in my bedroom. For the first time since I had arrived in Brussels I began to worry seriously as to where was that other agent whom I had requested should if possible keep me secret company. I had received no sign and had no idea where to look. So far I had got nothing out of my Colonel, and while he talked I was thinking to myself that I wanted the company of a friend very much.

As my eye wandered round the busy lounge an announcement of a Command Concert at the Opera House for that night suspended from a pillar caught my attention. I asked the Colonel to take me.

'Certainly, mein Fräulein,' he smiled. 'It is a good suggestion.' Then he stroked up his moustache and gazed naively at the ceiling. 'Music will be a fitting prelude to other delights,' he continued. 'Incidentally tonight at the Opera is a great gala night, for the All Highest will be present.'

My heart leaped. I determined that we should dine well that night, so well that wine should unlock his tongue. It did, but not to the extent that I had wanted. At the Opera there was a dense crowd of military men, but few civilians. When the All Highest entered and the orchestra crashed out 'Deutschland Uber Alles', all leaped to their feet like one great wave. Then followed prolonged cheering while the audience remained standing. I thought there sounded a note of artificiality in those cheers. The Kaiser took scant notice of the people all around him. As he listlessly sat back in his box among his glittering staff I detected a sad look on his face, as though bowed down by the weight of responsibility. And here was I, a spy, within a few yards of him, planning his death! The Colonel pressed my hand in the darkness of the box and I felt his lips brush my neck.

'Why do you look nowhere but at the All Highest, with that strange look in your eyes, my angel. Come, will you not pay a little attention to me?' he whispered, and it seemed to me that I started as though struck, but apparently he noticed nothing.

Back once more in the hotel we drank coffee and brandy in the lounge. My host leaned across the table. As he lit a match for his cigar his hand trembled. His breath smelt of alcohol, which was unusual for him. I looked away, not daring to think, and the disappointment of having been able to make him disclose nothing made it all seem so painfully futile. Soon now I should be alone with him and a German lieutenant at the next table but one deliberately winked at me and looked away. For a moment I did not understand. The Colonel was talking but I heard nothing. Was this perhaps my secret agent? Within a minute or two the lieutenant looked at me again, nodded faintly, got to his feet and walked to the lift.

'Come, little one,' suggested the Colonel rising a trifle unsteadily. 'You are perhaps tired. We will go to our room.'

Upstairs he took me in his arms.

'In a little while I shall return,' he told me, looking toward my night-dress which was laid out on the peacock-blue eiderdown, and he went out with a smile, gently closing the door behind him. I stared round the room, not knowing what to do next. Then I approached the window, let up the blind and gazed out on the calm night. Below in the depths ran a side-street, for my room was at the side of the hotel, and beyond stretched the roof-tops and spires of Brussels, rising so silent, gaunt, unsympathetic in the moonlight.

A little balcony lay outside my window and, opening it, I stepped through. The soft night wind ruffled my hair and seemed to give confidence to my burning senses. Suddenly a figure appeared upon the balcony next to mine. It was a man and he made a warning gesture with his hand. Only a few yards separated us. He slipped over the narrow space, gripped my rail, and in a moment we were standing peering into each other's faces.

I caught his hand and drew him into the light of the bedroom. It was the German lieutenant who had winked at me in the lounge, except that now he was clad in a black and scarlet brocaded dressing-gown beneath which I caught a glimpse of blue silk pyjamas. He grinned and smoothed crisp tousled hair. Then he lifted the lapel of his dressing-gown, showed me two diagonally placed safety-pins nestling there, and laughed.

'Good evening,' he murmured. 'I am an Englishman. I am on the Secret Intelligence in Brussels. There are several of us here. I daresay you were surprised to see me in a German uniform, but personally I was fitted into this job by our War Office before the war got started. We received warning of the important job you were on, and I was detailed to shadow you.'

'You recognised the violets and snowdrops without leaves?'

'Yes,' he nodded, and then took out his cigarette case, opened it, but suddenly, as an afterthought, shut it again sadly, 'S'pose I'd better not smoke,' he decided. 'Old Colonel might smell it when he came back. Look here, have you succeeded in getting anything out of him? Tell me, what can I do to assist?'

'So far I have been unable to learn anything, but perhaps I shall know something before tomorrow morning.' There was silence between us. 'To-night is going to be rather a difficult one for me,' I explained a little ruefully. He nodded, looking grave.

'I wish I could help you,' he said.

'You couldn't,' I assured him. 'It would only throw suspicion on both of us if you try to help me actively. I must rely on myself tonight. But here is where you can help. Suppose that I do manage to ascertain the information I want within time to make use of it, I intend to get back to Roulers immediately, as I can transmit the warning quicker direct over the frontier and thence by the regular channel to the Air authorities near the line than you would be able to do from here.'

'You may throw suspicion upon yourself by trying to run away,' he put in.

'I don't think so,' I replied. 'Why should he suspect me, and what could he prove even if he did? The line I shall take from now onwards is the frightened and virtuous young girl and that would be my excuse for running away. In any case I believe he would be somewhat anxious to keep my disappearance quiet from his friends, especially as he had no right to give me a special pass to Brussels in the first place. However, I continued, 'it is possible that I shall not be able to elude the Colonel. In that case, as a warning to you of this fact, I shall wear green leaves with the bunch of snowdrops and violets at my collar, and I shall place my message in the ring of the steel bracket which clamps the water-pipe to the wall between our two balconies.'

'I understand,' he rejoined, and then looked hard at the Colonel's two suitcases which still stood untouched where the soldier had placed them by the bed. 'Do those cases belong to your precious Colonel?' he enquired.

'Yes.'

'Have you searched them for papers?'

'Not yet.' He was down on his knees in a moment.

'Fortunately they are unlocked,' he muttered, hastily running his hand through the contents with the hand of an expert, so that he did not disturb them. He drew out a packet of papers and ran through them with swift eagerness. He selected three and pushed the rest back whence they came.

'Nothing of much value,' he grinned, removing one scarlet slipper and stuffing them inside. 'Better than nothing, all the same.'

He had one leg poised in the air as he replaced the slipper, when there sounded a rap on the door.

'The Colonel,' I gasped. Then the door-handle began to turn. I choked back a scream. Turning I saw nothing. The Lieutenant had vanished. But he could not possibly have escaped through the window in time. There were no cupboards for a man of his size. He had taken refuge beneath the bed.

The Colonel smiled a trifle vacantly, and then encircled me in his arms.

'You have not yet undressed, my angel,' he chided. 'Ah, but I see that you were about to unpack my cases,' he said, his gaze falling upon the two open suitcases which the Lieutenant had abandoned. His lips sought mine, while my mind was in a whirl. What could I do? I must play for time. Somehow I must give the Lieutenant a chance to slip over the balcony into his own room.

'I cannot stay here after tonight,' I whispered. 'I am frightened – besides, what will the Herr Oberartz say at the hospital if I am absent when the All Highest arrives? There are various duties in the hospital which are specially assigned to me and it is essential that I should be present.'

'Do not worry,' replied the Colonel, 'we have two days yet, and your leave can be extended. He arrives on Saturday to review the troops at 11 o'clock, and will afterwards inspect the place. He will not even stay the night, so that he will only take a cursory glance all round. I think that you could perfectly well stay away for the All Highest's visit altogether. What do you say, my sweet?'

So, at least I knew what I had set out to learn! 'I promised the Oberartz I would return,' I mumbled, hardly aware of what I was saying, for I was thinking feverishly of the man under my bed and what would happen if he were found. My lover held me close and pressed his lips on mine. I did not care, I was thinking, thinking furiously, desperately. In another room down the corridor German voices were singing. Sing – how could anybody in the world sing when such a ghastly dilemma was playing itself out in this bedroom?

Somebody was walking along the passage. Little did they think of what was being enacted in here. Suddenly there came a tremendous crash of glass, and then oaths followed by peals of unsteady laughter. The Colonel relaxed his hold, listening. In a second I was at the door, for whatever it might be it offered some momentary respite. Outside a blear-eyed Saxon officer of middle age swayed gently to and fro in an ecstasy of delight, and aimlessly brandished an empty wine-glass, in admonition of a silent waiter who was collecting heaps of shattered glass upon his tray. Crowded in a near-by doorway and peeping over each other's shoulders were the Saxon's comrades, applauding loudly. I hoped the Colonel would follow me out of the room, and so I rushed up to the gallant Saxon and asked what was the matter.

The officer stiffened and made an attempt at a bow which nearly over-balanced him, and then said: 'Believe me, the explanation is quite simple, Fräulein. This pig-dog and myself tried to pass in the passage, but as you see there was not room for such an intricate manoeuvre,' and his arm swept the passage, where at least five men could have walked abreast. 'Therefore,' he concluded, 'our momentum was such that we were unable to avoid a collision.' As he said these last words the Colonel, to my intense relief, looking somewhat surprised and annoyed, came out and joined us.

The Major knew the Colonel, as did several of the others, and after pre-liminary bows and heel-clicking of a rather unsteady kind, he was hailed cheerily and two full glasses were passed over the heads in the doorway, although not without spilling a good deal upon the said heads, and even-tually reached the Colonel and myself. Then everybody was talking, laughing and shouting, and the Colonel, because several of the officers there were senior to himself, had to remain a few minutes out of polite-ness. When nobody seemed to be looking in my direction I seized the momentary opportunity to slip back to my bedroom.

Here I double-locked the door and rushed to the bed. As I hoped, the Lieutenant had made his escape. One terrible crisis of that night had been got over, anyway. I was not sure what to do next, but I had not long to wait.

The Colonel was knocking on the door and fruitlessly turning the handle.

'Listen, my angel, I am waiting outside. Will you not let me in?' he was urging. 'Perhaps it is that you are undressing,' he said as an afterthought, 'and you would prefer that I wait?'

'Yes, I am undressing,' I told him breathlessly.

'Very well, I understand. I will rejoin you later, and go to my friends for one quarter of an hour. *Au revoir*, my dearest dear. We shall meet again very soon,' and I heard his footsteps recede up the corridor.

The drink I had gulped down in the other room must have been strong, for my brain was working with a bell-like clearness. All of a sudden, I knew exactly what I was going to do. I would run from the hotel immediately, while the Colonel was in the other room. I had all the information I had wanted. As for my suitcase with the few spare clothes I had brought with me, that could go hang. There was nothing which could incriminate me.

With the help of my railway pass I should be able to catch a train before dawn for Roulers, and once I was outside the hotel and in public I did not think the Colonel would pursue and cause a scene for reasons I have mentioned.

I scribbled in pencil on a piece of writing-paper:

HERR COLONEL
I reserve the right of a woman to change her mind. I was a young and foolish girl; I was carried away by you. Now I am going home, and I hope eventually you will forgive me.
  Good-bye.
  MARTHA

Then seizing my special railway pass and the key of the door, for I had decided to relock it on the outside and keep the key to perplex the Colonel for a few extra minutes while the distance between us widened as much as possible, I tore open the door and dashed straight into the solid grey form which blocked the way. It was the Colonel.

He smiled down at me and explained a little thickly: 'My angel, I have just remembered that when I was holding you in my arms in our bedroom, I heard my cigar case drop to the floor from my breeches pocket. I had come to ask that you would hand it out to me, angel, for I loathe other men's cheap cigars; but, behold, here you come to meet me!' Suddenly the significance of the fact that I was still fully dressed seemed to penetrate his fuddled senses, and he may have noticed the wild min my face.

'What is the matter, mein Fräulein?' he interrogated, holding me by the shoulders and gently forcing me back through the door. 'Where do you go?'

'Please let me go,' I breathed. 'I have changed my mind. I am leaving for home. Please, please – but forgive me. I am frightened, I ought never to have come. I was mad, crazy, but please let me go!' I tried to slip from his grasp, but he held me firmly, though not unkindly.

'Little one, little one, there is nothing at which to be frightened. Calm yourself. Sit down and I will fetch you a drink.' He kissed my forehead tenderly, and I leaned away from him as far as I could as I looked around me wildly, feeling my last chance of escape had gone.

In an alcove of the wall beside the door stood the washhand stand with the basin and ewer of gleaming blue china. I looked up at the Colonel. He was neither intoxicated nor sober. He was not very steady, and I did not think his brain would work quickly. I let my body lie limp against his, with my head resting near his shoulder, then in a flash, I braced my limbs and leaped back with all my strength. I reached the washhand stand, and seizing the blue ewer, launched the whole contents full into the Colonel's eyes before he understood what was happening. He staggered back gasping, and just behind him, as I had calculated, were the two suitcases by the bed-foot. I rushed at him and threw all the weight of my body into a sudden shove. He toppled headlong backwards over the cases and I think his had struck the copper knob of the bedpost.

I turned and catching up my train pass and the door-key had fallen to the floor, fled from my peacock bedroom, locking the door behind me.

A moment later I was hastening through the darkened and deserted lounge. The night doorkeeper wished me a polite good night. It was no business of his, but for all that he must have wondered where a lady guest in the hotel was going at that hour.

One hour and a half later I was lying back in the train, still breathless and incredulous, gliding swiftly through the night towards Roulers.

It was growing late when the train drew into Roulers. A woman passenger on the trains at that time was unusual, but my pass carried me safely through the military police at the barrier. Everybody was still in bed when I reached the café, but presently my mother was embracing me in the doorway. She did not question me as to where I had been. It was enough for her that I had returned safely.

'"Canteen Ma" called here yesterday and left this,' she told me, sipping a cheap pincushion into my hands. The message read: 'No. 63 is absent on a special mission until Thursday. If before that day you have urgent news to transmit you must yourself carry the information to the Van Root's farmhouse along the Thourout-Roulers Road. You will knock at the door with two short and three long raps and hand your message to a fat woman (with a florid complexion) within. You will not allude to the message in any way, but will greet all as acquaintances.'

I knew of the Van Roots, trustworthy folk who lived at a lonely farmstead among pine-trees lying nearby the highway. But the distance from Roulers was about 15 miles by road, and as I could not risk using such a conspicuous route, it meant a journey of almost 20 miles by night over rough countryside. I should have to leave Roulers as soon as darkness fell and make all haste for my destination. The Overartz must not know of my return to Roulers until after I had come back from delivering my message. I should have overstayed my leave, but I could excuse myself on the grounds of my imaginary grandmother's extreme illness and the fact that I had heard in Brussels that the All Highest would not visit us until Saturday.

I left Roulers at 10 o'clock that Wednesday night in a shower of rain and inky blackness. I had only a small torch to guide me and could wear neither coat nor hat, as anyone who had the appearance of having travelled any distance in those days was immediately under suspicion. One always had to look as though one were just running in to see a neighbour, whatever was the real nature of the mission. Food, shelter and if necessary a hiding-place could always be found with Belgians whose homesteads were *en route*, and no questions were ever asked or information ever given to prying German gendarmes, who both in uniform and plain clothes were sometimes to be met with in unexpected places. All along the route to the frontier was a string of farms, private houses, empty ruins and factories which formed a veritable network of relays for the runners with secret and vital information. Here, also, fugitives bound for Holland might lie safely hidden for months. It is when I remember these things, and the unselfish, fearless spirit that was manifested in those war days, that I feel proud of my countrymen.

The old town was only a mile behind me when the moon suddenly glided from behind a cloud, plunging the deserted landscape into a sea of light and shadow. The drizzle ceased and I felt the warmness of the night, but the rain had made the ground slippery and sodden, and the way was wild and strewn with small undulations. I had to break my way through hedges, and sometimes had to crawl through ditches, keeping a watchful eye for prowling figures. It was a terribly tiring business, but I cannot honestly say that I disliked it. Once only I saw human beings, and that was when I was crossing a road. It was at a bend where the hedges were high and the road was dark with trees. As I was in the middle of the road an approaching light appeared round the bend. I hurled myself into the water-logged ditch as a gendarme bicycle patrol swept round the corner.

It was 6.00am by my watch when I came on an old house standing by itself, where a light was flickering in the lower windows. I was not certain of the way, so I called at the door to enquire. The aged woman who answered my knock showed no surprise at my muddy, bedraggled condition. She said not a word, but took my hand and led me in, patting my wrist softly. She gave me steaming hot coffee and bread and butter by the fire and then directed me onwards.

When I had walked three-quarter way up the stone-flagged mien path of the Van Roots' homestead I suddenly noticed beside the wooden porch two muddy bicycles. They were German military bicycles. My heart stood still, and I thought of retracing my steps. Then it occurred to me that to do so would be indiscreet as I might already have been observed from the windows. I advanced boldly to the door as though it was quite a natural thing to be smothered in mud from head to foot, but I thought it prudent to knock on the door like a chance caller and not to use the preconcerted signal. The red-faced fat woman herself opened the door and I greeted her loudly like an old friend. The passage behind her was empty, so I quietly rapped out the signal on the door-panel. She nodded, and I passed the note into her hand.

'It shall go immediately,' she said, when she saw the 'Urgent' with which I had marked it. She glanced over her shoulder. 'Two gendarmes on night patrol called here for food,' she told me. 'They are washing in the scullery. You must come upstairs before they see you, and hide among the rafters.'

I stretched myself in the straw of the loft and fell fast asleep. An hour later she told me I might safely come down. After a square meal, which I took basking at a table in the sunbathed garden, she helped me indoors, washed me in a hip-bath like a small child; during which process I several times fell asleep; and having taken my garments to be brushed and dried, she led me to a feather-bed, into which I slipped blissfully, and closed my eyes.

At 10 o'clock that night I started for home. I had determined to spend the next day with friends who lived half-way to Roulers, and to complete the journey the following night. Thus I calculated I could be home at 4.30am on the Saturday morning, and would have ample time to present myself at the hospital at my usual hour of 7 o'clock.

As I set out to the hospital that Saturday morning the air was fresh and enlivening, the birds sang merrily and the sun shone in a blue sky. I thought of the All Highest sitting silently in his opera box, and wondered if today was to be his last. The streets were festooned with gay flags in honour of his coming.

Alphonse was tinkering with the wheel of an ambulance before the steps in the courtyard as I approached. He looked at me searchingly, for although he could not have known where I had been, he may have had a pretty shrewd idea.

'Good morning, sister,' he began. 'Have you heard the news; it has just been received. The Kaiser is not coming to visit us after all. For the last few days the "Seven Sisters" have flown over and bombed us regularly, so they have decided that it will be too dangerous for him.'

I said nothing, for there was really nothing to be said.

CHAPTER EIGHT

SECRET SERVICE DAYS

By Edwin T. Woodhall

When war broke out my only brother and I both joined up. It seemed strange that I should go safely through some of the fiercest engagements, yet that my brother should be killed in his first attack. His name can be seen on the beautiful Cenotaph between St Lawrence and Ramsgate – 'Samuel Woodhall, age 41, killed in action.'

The first shots between the Germans and English, when they came face to face as enemies for the first time in modern history, took place at twenty minutes to one on the afternoon of Sunday, 24 August 1914, and from that period onward to 6 September my brigade was constantly in action.

An incident of 1914 days which will remain impressed upon my memory concerns the two late Field-Marshals of the British Army – the Earl of Ypres and Earl Haig, then Sir John French and Sir Douglas Haig.

It was on the first day of our retirement, in face of the German hordes, amidst terrific heat and dust, when, with a few men of my brigade, I went into a large yard of a deserted farm for the purpose of filling water-bottles.

To our astonishment we saw the Union Jack, and in a large dust-covered car the Commander-in-Chief. Standing close by, and in deep silence, was a group of officers who, irrespective of the white dust covering them from head to foot, were obviously of high staff rank.

Their faces, like those of the troops staggering by outside, were grime-covered, unshaven and haggard, with eyes sunken and hollow from want of sleep.

We instinctively turned to go back to the road outside, when one beckoned me towards him, and, as I came near, I at once recognised the handsome features of Sir Douglas Haig, 1st Army Commander.

'What do you boys want?' he asked in lowered tones. Saluting, I replied: 'Only water, sir, if there's any to be got.'

'Yes,' he answered. 'There's a pump round there. Take what you want, but, for the love of Heaven, get it quietly. Make no noise – your

Commander-in-Chief has been asleep for five minutes – the first he has had for nearly four days.'

As I passed by on my way to the pump I saw Sir John French lying back in the corner of his car – asleep.

To others, as well as myself, the incident conveyed all that our leaders had to endure. The strain on the men was terrible, but who can fully realise the ordeal which these great soldiers passed in the darkest hours of our Nation's history?

I served with my regiment from Mons to the Marne, from the Aisne to Flanders, and in 1915, by the instructions of my commanding officer, Sir Philip Robinson, DSO, KCB, MVO, was transferred to the counter-espionage department of the Intelligence Department, Secret Service. This meant a position of responsibility and opportunity for adventure, which was all to my liking.

It does not need much imagination on the part of anyone who was present in France in those days to picture how arduous was our work in the Intelligence Department.

The country was teeming with German hirelings and spies of all kinds. We had to keep constant vigilance for mysterious lights, pigeon-flying, suspects in British and French uniform, and scrutinise and inquire into the credentials of all civilian labourers working behind the lines. The tricks, resources, and ramifications of the German Secret Service were legion.

For instance, on one occasion a French soldier in uniform on leave came into the town of Estaires with his aged father. Questioned as to what they were doing behind the British lines, in the zone of the armies, they produced their *laisser-passer* and said that they wished to visit their former home to see if they could discover a small hoard of money hidden during the first onrush of the German armies.

The Town Major, or British Assistant Provost-Marshal, accepted their version and gave them the necessary authority to proceed to their native village, a shell-blasted derelict place inhabited only by British Artillery observation officers, and within incessant gun-fire of the German lines, also in the immediate rear of the British and Canadian section of trenches. I happened to call upon the Town Major that day, having just come through on a commission from the 3rd Corps Army Headquarters. In fact, as I alighted from my Triumph motor cycle, our friend and his aged parent came out of his office.

I knocked at his door, saluted and entered. He knew me.

'Good morning, Sergeant,' he said.

'Good morning, sir,' I answered. 'Anything my way to-day?'

'No.' he replied. 'One or two lights at night; but the Town Guard saw to that.'

We continued to talk, and I asked him quite casually who were the old man and his son. When he told me, I was suspicious at once. In fact, right throughout my Secret Service days I fostered a dual nature, for I suspected, in the exigencies of my work, everything and everybody until satisfied.

'You'll excuse me, sir,' I said, 'but I think you have exceeded your duty. I shall report this incident to Army Headquarters.'

I did not wait for his reply, but dashed off out and on to my 'bike'.

It did not take me long to overtake them, and dismounting I saluted the French soldier and said:

'Pardon, I am a sergeant of the English Military Police. Show me your military book!'

He explained that he had come on leave; in fact, repeated exactly what the Major had previously told me, and everything appeared to be in order, but, just to be on the safe side, they were closely watched – so much so that though they were afterwards found to be 'suspect' by the French authorities, they did not, on that occasion, attempt to carry out their scheme, whatever it was, and had to stick to their assumed role. The result of my report to headquarters was a transfer of the Town Major and an immediate tightening up all round, the Army Brigade and Divisional Provosts-Marshal being the only authorities to issue permits of any description.

With regard to the Allied Secret Service, I state emphatically it was far superior to that of the German.

In real military Secret Service work there is only one set of people who can be relied on, and they are the military spies who act out of purely patriotic motives, and whom I would term, for the want of a better definition, 'national spies'.

The French displayed much daring, resource and intrepid bravery in work of this description, and to quote Colonel W. Nicolai (Chief of the German Secret Service) will, I think, be the best example of what I am trying to convey:

'In 1915 nine "air spies" – four in uniform – and five aeroplanes fell into our hands. Attempts to pick up the spies again were watched. The French aeroplanes would fly at the arranged time over the landing-place, kept under observation by German counter-espionage agents. But the airmen in such cases flew at a considerable height, because the sign agreed upon that the coast was clear was not given. In no case was it definitely ascertained that an "air spy" was really taken off again.

'Some were caught far behind the front in Eastern Belgium. They were instructed that if they reached Holland they were to report to the French Consul, who would see to their return to France.

'Some of them had instructions to destroy railway lines and bridges in the rear of the German army, especially in those parts of the front in which a German attack was expected or an Allied offensive was to take place.

'*Regarding successful enterprises of this nature nothing can be ascertained.*

'The usefulness of air spies lay mainly in the information they sent by their carrier pigeons.

'This method of obtaining information could not be resorted to by the German military authorities. *No enemy prisoners of war were found who would undertake work of this nature against their own country.*'

In respect of bravery displayed by the enemy, they were our equal, but they suffered from being in enemy territory, with inhabitants favourable to the Allies. They tried our methods, but I do not think, from a military point of view, they had the success of the Allies.

I recall seeing the shattered body of a spy near Albert in 1916. He had been dropped from an enemy aeroplane during the night, but his parachute had failed to act. He had given his life for the Fatherland with fortitude as did our own brave men for their cause.

We certainly had much trouble in those days with some French and Belgian civilians working in the pay of the enemy.

Lieutenant E.H. King, Intelligence Officer of my Brigade arrested a man named Debacker-Polydore, of Croix de Bac, in the act of cutting our telegraph wires with a pair of insulated pliers.

He was tried by the French Civil and Military Authorities, found guilty, and shot as a spy on 11 November, 1914.

These, it is perhaps needless to say, being inhabitants of the parts in which they operated, were far more difficult to deal with than were German members of the Huns' Secret Service who had crossed the lines for the purpose of espionage. I do not think many got back. In fact, towards 1917, our Intelligence Department had become so efficient that it was almost an impossibility for any civilian in the zone of the armies to move without his every movement being accounted for and recorded.

Pigeons upon both sides played quite an important part during the war. The Germans often used them to send into various secret homing lofts in the Allied territories, or, on the other hand, back to different parts of the occupied territories in Germany.

I have dealt with cases of enemy pigeons in many parts of the British line, some having alighted by reason of mating instinct, exhaustion, or wounds.

Dogs, also, were used by both sides, and in cases of attack could be trained to advantage. Some of these dumb animals showed remarkable intelligence, and conveyed, backwards and forwards, repeatedly in the face of death, very valuable information.

Paddy, the dear little mongrel dog whose life-story at some future time I intend to write, is only one of the many dumb Secret Service agents that worked for the belligerents upon both sides during the war.

In the first months of hostilities it was much easier, and often, too, innocent civilians became entangled in the machinations of spies without knowing it, as witness the case of the old lady of Fleurbaix.

In the early days of the war I had occasion to be in the neighbourhood of this village, and, owing to my duty, had been keeping watch at certain cross-roads for something entirely different from that which I am about to relate.

On two evenings I saw an old peasant woman pass me at about the same time, so, on the third evening, I considered it strange.

On the fourth evening I kept out of sight, but observed that the old lady passed just as before and in the same direction. Having decided to keep watch and satisfy myself about her, I discovered that she invariably entered a partly-ruined church at about seven in the evening, always carrying a little basket.

Evening after evening I discovered this performance to be a regular thing, so I decided to act. She entered the church, went straight to a door in the tower, and began to mount the shell-smashed stairs. Up she went, muttering and mumbling in Flemish, and at last reached the top storey.

She had no idea that I was close behind her, and when I confronted her she was in the act of handing provisions from her basket to an officer in British uniform.

For a moment I was nonplussed, but, realising that I must go on, I demanded to know who he was, and what he was doing there under such peculiar circumstances.

With great indignation, he replied: 'What do you "vont" to know for?'

That was enough. I whipped out my revolver and covered him. He asked if I had gone crazy, and threatened all sorts of punishments; and I must admit he nearly bluffed me – but that little word 'vont' for 'want' was, I instinctively knew, the mark of the Teuton.

His statement was that he was attached to the 'X' Battery and was then on duty as observation officer.

Determined to see it through, I made him precede me downstairs and asked him to accompany me to his commanding officer.

It was then that the truth came out.

He was a German officer, though speaking English almost perfectly. He had been for ten days in the tower and had communicated the movements of our troops by means of a field-telephone, purposely left by the Germans when driven out of the village. When it appeared that he could bluff no longer, he became quite candid.

'You were lucky,' he said. 'In another six hours I should have been back across the lines.'

He smiled as he added: 'The fortune of war!'

The poor old woman was quite an innocent factor. She had been asked by this officer during one of his night expeditions to bring him a daily supply of food, and, thinking him British, and entirely ignorant of military law, she had complied.

The spy, it transpired, had been the manager of a well-known London hotel, and had been recalled to the German flag in July, 1914.

I never knew how he ended, but I do not think we shot him. He was taken away by car for interrogation, and, I believe, interned.

My last impression of him was seated in a large Rolls-Royce car between two armed officers *en route* for an unknown destination. As the car moved off, his fine blue eyes met mine. I smiled and saluted. Yes! a brave man. But he was a spy against my country.

On 22 November 1916, in full view of thousands of mud-grimed soldiers, who watched the combat from their trenches, took place one of the most deadly aerial combats of the War.

It was between Manfred von Richthofen, Germany's crack ace, and Captain Hawker, at that time the most daring and intrepid English airman in the Royal Flying Corps.

Both men, respectively, had a long list of enemy deaths upon their escutcheons of fame and both, as great belligerent champions, were destined one day to meet.

It was a duel between two highly-experienced enemy leaders for the recognised supremacy. Like two fighting eagles, they circled and man-oeuvred around each other to gain the vital advantage, and the memory of this sight will remain with me for all time.

With a strong pair of glasses I watched from a forward artillery officer's observation post near Albert the last encircling aerial evolution of the English plane. By this time Hawker had driven Richthofen well over the German lines towards Bapaume, and from what I could gather, they were going around and around each other in swift and ever-narrowing circles, both playing for the position of target with their machine-guns.

To this day I can never account for it. Perhaps it was some curious optical illusion – but it seemed to happen in a second – suddenly the

German red Fokker was behind the English plane spitting machine-gun fire – 50 yards from behind the tail of Hawker's machine.

With a roaring glide I saw the English machine race earthward toward the German lines – and that was the last seen of one of the greatest English airmen.

Let me add in passing that Baron Manfred von Richthofen, whom I saw upon many occasions in aerial combat with the Allies, has been admitted to be the greatest aerial 'Ace' of the world.

Up to the day of his death, 21 April 1918, near the lines of the Thirty-third Australian Field Battery, 5th Division, between Sailley-le-Sec, not far from Corbie, on the Somme, he had brought down no fewer than eighty of the Allied aeroplanes.

He took toll upon English, French, and Americans, among whose names are to be found Hawker, Ball, McCudden, Immelmaan, Guynemer, Lugberry and Quintin Roosevelt.

A well-known American journalist, Mr Floyd Gibbon, attributes the death of Richthofen to the machine-gun fire of Captain Roy Brown, who came up behind while the German was pursuing another English airman named Lieutenant May.

May, with Richthofen roaring behind him, was racing from death with no ammunition. He was planing down in a race towards the British trenches. Near the Australian lines the machines could not have been more than 100 yards apart – and some of the 'Diggers' were firing on the Red Fokker of the German.

Suddenly Captain Brown, from out of the blue as it were, and behind Richthofen, swooped down – and up – releasing as he did so a deadly volley into the cockpit of the Fokker beneath.

Officially, the RFC claim the Red Knight of Germany's death – but to this day the surviving witnesses of the 5th Australian Division claim that a shot from one of their men had already killed the Baron before Captain Brown swooped down upon him from behind.

In a large marquee tent the body of Richthofen lay in state behind the British lines for two or three days prior to its interment.

Thousands of officers from all parts of the Allied front came to see the remains of this daring German airman.

In burying him with full military honours, the British paid the highest tribute possible to the memory of a gallant foe.

Another recollection of the War – and one of the most treasured – goes back to the period when the Heir-Apparent, our beloved Prince of Wales, was attached to the General Staff in France.

His known contempt for danger and his habit of 'looking for trouble' were a constant source of anxiety to the high officers responsible for his safety.

The method of guarding the Prince was for his 'shadower' to assume various roles which would render him inconspicuous. Mine usually was that of a dispatch rider.

Often it was quite impossible to keep him in sight, and there were many times when Headquarters received a nasty shock because the Prince was missing.

On one occasion it was suddenly realised that the Prince had not been seen for some time, and, although enquiries were immediately instituted, nobody seemed to know where he had gone.

The first knowledge that I had of the trouble was when I was approached by several Staff Officers in a long communication trench. They were breathless with hurrying, and were obviously in a state of great anxiety.

One of them recognised me, and a look of relief came over his face as he said: '*Oh, here's the Intelligence Police chap, perhaps he can tell us something.*'

I could and I did. I had been trailing the Prince for hours, and at the time during which Headquarters were in a mortal funk lest something should have happened to him, the Prince was in the corner of a machine-gun emplacement, talking to a young lieutenant, some sergeants, and a big bunch of interested Tommies.

Can it be wondered that he is so beloved by us all?

He said: 'I found my manhood in France,' and never was a truer and more sincere speech uttered. First and foremost he is a man and a Prince afterwards.

It was not long after this that there occurred an incident which might have robbed the Throne of its heir.

I was waiting for him to set out on one of his daily pilgrimages when suddenly I saw a high-powered car drive up to the headquarters at Merville. It was clear that he was going up the line, and it was equally clear that he would be going at a pace with which it would be impossible for me to keep up on my bike, good engine though it had.

I hung on as long as I possibly could, but at length lost sight of the car altogether.

However, I carried on until I got well into the danger zone, and the German artillery were putting over some very heavy stuff. I pulled up and made some enquiries of a few Tommies, and through this medium I managed to pick up the trace of the Prince and set off in the direction where he had been last seen. It was in the artillery area and in the very heart of a shell-blasted region.

At that moment a terrible roar and crash indicated the explosion of a shell on a derelict farm about 400 yards to my front, and I hurried on.

Suddenly, I came upon the Prince standing near to a wall, looking shaky and distinctly pale. And small wonder. It appears that he had left his car in what he considered to be a place of comparative shelter – that is to say, he had left it protected by a thick wall that had been left standing.

He had gone out a little way, and, on his return, was horrified to find that both the wall and the car had been blown to atoms.

A few seconds earlier, and he would have been killed.

More than once (he got to know me and spoke to me often) I have detected a gleam of amusement in his eyes when he caught sight of me. I have seen him glance round at me with a little smile as much as to say:

'So you still insist on shadowing me. Right, old chap! I'll give you a run for your money. By the time I've finished with you and my walk across country, you'll be glad to get back on that old motor-bike of yours!'

II

Later on in the war I was transferred to Boulogne, Paris, and Le Havre, and at the last-named place not only met with adventures, but came into contact with a number of interesting persons and became acquainted with numerous secrets of espionage. Of the latter I could tell many stories which I am not at liberty to set down at the moment.

I have only one recollection of the subject of the Intelligence Police Department having been touched upon before, and that was by Sir Basil Thomson, late Assistant Commissioner, New Scotland Yard, in his book entitled *Queer People*.

He refers to the department only very briefly, inasmuch as he states how the nucleus of the Intelligence Police was formed in the initial stages of war, how it was made up, and the type of personnel.

I will go farther and state that I consider the brunt of the main work of prevention and detection of espionage in France at this time was con-ducted by Lieutenant-Colonel I.S. Knox Lamb, OBE, and many other officers, including Captain Priestly, DSO, who was in command, at my time, of Le Havre Base.

The former distinguished officer was fortunate in having at his disposal such clever and brilliant police detectives, loaned from Headquarters London Metropolitan Police, as M. Clancy, A. Canning, W. Selby, A. Lander, P. Worth, P. Smith, I. Brown, W. Tireback, C. Kite, Trevet

Reid, T. Hunson, C. Frost, Inspector Burt, and the late Inspectors E. Hill and Leo Gough.

Attached to these experienced men was another section of capable auxiliaries who augmented the Intelligence Police on the Lines of Communication and Army Areas, and were drawn from the best class of educated British manhood procurable.

All of them were efficient linguists and comprised such types as stockbrokers, partners of big business houses, civil, mechanical, and electrical engineers, artists, journalists, surveyors, accountants, men of travel-men of good family, men of the world. In fact, the finest types and the best brains obtainable, judiciously selected and trained to play their part to combat the machinations of the enemy's espionage system.

My main duties at Le Havre were at the 'Gare des Voyageurs,' the main arrival and departure station for Rouen and Paris. I was attached to the French Commissaire Special, and my primary duties consisted of examination of all persons travelling with British passports, while the French detectives were responsible for all passports of other nationalities.

By certain pre-arranged visas or markings, I knew who were suspect and who were otherwise. The code was known to all members of the Intelligence Police, and although specific instructions were issued in regard to such, each Intelligence Police member acted on his own initiative and responsibility in determining his line of action in any unforeseen contingency.

The French Detective Chief, or Commissaire Special, was, during my tenure of office, one Monsieur Caserne, under whom were about a dozen or so detectives of various ranks and grades.

Working with them all – these French officials – with their respective personalities, temperaments and mannerisms, remains one of my great experiences, and the memory of certain individuals lingers tenderly in my mind. In the presence of any known superior or anyone they deemed of importance, I was *Le Serjent Woodhall*. I fraternised with superiors and subordinates and was secretly designated 'Monsieur Ted,' my Christian name. This, coming from a body of Frenchmen, who are sticklers for etiquette, showed their friendly appraisement of their foreign comrade.

All travellers to and from Paris, or crossing either way the French, Spanish, Swiss, or Italian frontiers, via Southampton and Le Havre, came through my hands, and many and numerous were the strange duties, incidents, and irregularities which cropped up.

Ambassadors, diplomatic couriers, King's messengers, special messengers, naval and military attachés and officers of high rank, big commercial magnates – in fact, all, from the highest to the lowest, passed through my hands.

I handled, through my control barrier, the passports and special papers of many distinguished people. On one occasion the late Field-Marshal Lord Kitchener, in mufti, came through, as also did Mr Winston Churchill. Of course, no control was necessary in the case of such persons of national importance. Facility of progress was the order in that case.

The late Master of Elibank, Lord Murray, came through, and our recognition was mutual. I saw him to his compartment and we had a long chat with each other. He spoke of the old election days when I was attached to Mr David Lloyd George, and recounted many instances which caused us both amusement. His death a few years ago removed a distinguished man from public affairs.

Joe Childs, jockey to His Late Majesty, King George came through my control on his way from France to England, prior to joining up in the fighting forces. I recall him quite vividly, a charming, quiet, and gentlemanly little fellow.

We had many laughs together during his sojourn in Le Havre – and if his eyes meet these lines he will smile at a certain incident known only to him and me!

One day there was handed into my custody at the Gare des Voyageurs a man whom I will call 'A'.

He had been arrested by the French when crossing from Spain into France but, being an Englishman, had been sent to us to deal with.

At the time of his arrest his passports were in a muddle. I believe he had foolishly been trying to alter them himself. It was also learnt that he had been trying to get into communication with his wife, who was then in Brussels. His own actions had brought suspicion upon him and the case looked very grave.

When handed over to me he was in a dishevelled state, looked absolutely worn out and emaciated; his clothes were dirty and torn, he had no collar or hat, and was, in fact, a pitiable object. I could see that under normal conditions he was a superior type of man.

As he was handed into my custody by the detective of the French Sûreté Générale, his relief was great. His first words were: 'Thank God, I am in English hands at last!'

It was my duty to bring him over to England and hand him to the authorities at Southampton. This I did, being locked in the cabin with him on the steamer, and, during the trip, he told me much of what he had been through.

Brutally treated, he had been convinced that the French intended to shoot him. In England he had a square deal, eventually joined the forces and served with distinction. Today he occupies a high position in the journalistic and photographic world.

In the heights round about Le Havre were many encampments of German prisoners, guarded and maintained in some cases by the French. But the majority of detachments were under English control.

Nearly all the prisoners worked on the quays, loading and unloading the many ocean-going vessels arriving and departing with cargoes. The particular detachment of prisoners to which I refer was comprised of the Prussian Cavalry Guard, from which complement several successful escapes took place in spite of the strongest guard and the utmost vigilance exercised.

Collusion was suspected, and the French Military, to whom this detachment belonged, applied for secret assistance. I was deputed for the commission, and my instructions were 'Trace the source from which the prisoners get their instructions and assistance.'

In conjunction with the French Mobile Sûreté Général I took on my new task; in fact, I lost my identity. From a Sergeant of Intelligence my new role was as follows: A 'réforme Anglais' (English discharged soldier) living in Paris and married to a French woman, according to story, but working as a civilian labourer under the French people.

My first job was to get into the detachment under observation. This I did by applying for a position as crane-driver, realising that in this capacity I should have a better opportunity of watching without being suspected. Along the quayside there were many Belgian, French, and civilian labourers who, under the instructions of French officers, assisted the German prisoners in their tasks: of course, all under military guard.

My luck was in. I was taken as a crane-driver by the French civilian foreman on the strength of my 'Permis de Sejour' (Authority of local residence) and duly installed.

Naturally, I was instructed by a French crane-driver in the arts of an electrically driven crane, which, on the first day caused great amusement to the Germans and very nearly terminated my tenure on this earth.

My driving cabin was entered 8 feet from the ground, by an iron ladder.

The crane itself, being electrically controlled, had a huge arm shooting out from its centre with a large chain running up and down into the holds of any vessels or barges.

It also went round from left to right on an immense circular base. Also it could be moved on metal lines in the same direction if and when the case necessitated it.

I remember there was a switch to make the crane swing round. Left to left, right to right, and a lever which you plugged in to hoist and drop the chain, and another lever to send the whole crane along.

I soon picked up the principle and bade fair to become an excellent crane-driver. The only thing that needed dexterity of touch was the crane when it went round. Too much current would swing it instantly round and if – as it was that day – unloading heavy stuff, in this particular instance it was iron plates, the crane could be easily thrown off the cog wheels of its circular base on which it revolved by the swinging momentum of its load.

The afternoon was wearing on as I hoisted and dropped my tons of iron from shore to hold. I had just got the signal from the German officer to hoist from the ground to the ship, which was done, and as the iron load stood out on the end of the suspending chain slowly revolving in mid-air over the heads of the prisoners beneath, my eyes caught a slight movement on the part of a civilian and a German officer prisoner.

At the same time as I saw the movement – a swift passage of something which looked like paper – the civilian's eyes looked up and met mine! For the moment I thought he had detected me, and, in order to cover up any suspicion on his part I accidentally 'yanked' round the switch instead of the lever to lower the load into the hold.

Instantly the crane swung round, and just as quickly I switched back into neutral. The cabin rocked, men flew in all directions and I had a momentary glimpse of about ten tons of iron swinging madly backwards and forwards at the end of my chain hoist.

I shut my eyes, for, had it swung off its base, a 50-ton crane, including its driver, would have been precipitated into about 30 feet of water of the dock.

The crane stopped. I had switched off all current, more by luck than judgment. From below I could see the German prisoners, some laughing, others looking in amazement, and, above all, the voice of the French civilian foreman shouting out. 'Nom de Dieu!' 'Nom de Dieu!' 'Quelle affaire.' 'Quelle affaire.'

The foreman yelled on me to come out, which I did – and he promptly cursed me in his best French, and, to use an Americanism, 'I was fired!'

Ignominiously as I was treated, my purpose was served. I knew my man and in due course proceeded to track him. As he left work I shadowed him home, and left the rest to my French detective colleague.

As a result of my efforts I was informed that through the instrumentality of this particular Belgian labourer – a pure 'hireling' – a huge scheme organised from Berlin through Geneva and Paris was discovered by the French Sûreté Général.

At any rate during the whole period afterwards not another German escaped. The French saw to that! What became of the man I discovered handing over his message, I never knew. The French moved silently, but sometimes with deadly effect.

Upon another occasion I was loaned to the Admiralty. The trouble this time was a mysterious light seen by some of our Naval Patrol Boats outside the port of Le Havre.

It was alleged to be a clear flash to sea in the form of a Morse code, and it was conjectured that some enemy agent was signalling to a hidden submarine. Therefore, one afternoon, off I went by the ferry from Le Havre to Honfleur, that beautiful old-world town situated in the Commune of Calvados on the mouth of the Siene and opposite to Le Havre.

My orders were to report to the Senior Naval Commander, who at that time had a shore billet on the heights overlooking the Siene and the English Channel. He was a splendid specimen of typical Naval officer.

We discussed the question of the light and he admitted that it seemed too strange to be believed, in view of all the precautions taken by the French and English authorities.

I decided to stay for a few nights and investigate. Near to his bungalow, and on the top of the hill looking out to sea, was a small farm occupied by an old woman whose two sons were serving in the French Army. Her sole means of support were several cows which she turned out for grazing in the fields around her homestead. Assisting the old lady was an individual of apparently feeble intellect.

As the lights, which appeared every evening just after sundown, seemed, according to the information, to come from this direction, I was at a loss to understand.

On the third day I asked the Commander if the light had still been seen, and he assured me that it had. So I decided to watch the farm. It was getting near night-fall when I observed the half-witted man come out of the cottage. The cows were outside lowing to enter their shed for the night.

Judge my astonishment when I beheld the old lady leave the farm door and enter the cowshed. Swinging in her hand was a lighted hurricane lamp. I watched her enter the shed and busy herself with the cattle, all the time passing and re-passing with the lamp. *Suddenly the mystery of the light was solved.*

Turning round I could perceive that from the little farm the view out to sea was absolutely uninterrupted.

I reported accordingly, and the experiment was tried. Next evening at night-fall from out at sea keen eyes were watching – but the light was never seen again, because the Commander had informed the local gendarme, with the result that when the old lady required a light she took good care to see that it was not exposed to view.

There was absolutely no ulterior motive, the old lady in rural simplicity never realising her actions. When informed that an exposed light on a high eminence looking out to sea might give cause for much official perturbation, she quite innocently replied that it had been her custom for many years and this was the first time any complaint had ever been made against her!

We left the local gendarme to reprimand her, and there ended an episode which, like many more of a similar nature, turned out to be quite harmless in its foundation.

In 1917 I was transferred from the Intelligence Police to the Military Police at Etaples to assist in the rounding-up of deserters. I arrived at a period when this tremendous base depot, the largest reinforcement camp in France, situated about 20 miles or so from Boulogne, was settling down to comparative quietness. Sometime previously a first detachment of WAACs had arrived.

The Military Police at that time was comprised of a peculiarly assorted body of men, tact and experience apparently being the least sought-for qualification.

It would appear that a quarrel took place one night between a 'Tommy' and a Lance-Corporal of the Military Police. The subject was one of the WAACs. The row occurred through jealousy and terminated fatally, the 'Tommy' being shot – I believe accidentally – in the struggle.

Immediately the news flew round the huge camp, and the troops rose *en masse*.

'The Military Police! The 'Red-Caps'. Down with 'em!'

And nothing would have prevented a terrible riot had it not been for the presence of mind and wonderful tact displayed by several members of the Headquarters General Staff.

For days the trouble seethed, but in the end it simmered down to normal.

From this time onwards the Military Police was improved by the introduction into its ranks of non-commissioned officers made up mostly of policemen from all parts of the United Kingdom.

Two very popular and certainly the most efficient Military Police officers this difficult area ever had in command were Major Pym and Captain Cross. The former being Provost, and the latter Assistant

Provost, they commanded wisely, diplomatically, and firmly. At any rate, that was the unanimous opinion, so I think I am at liberty to quote what was considered to be the case.

In passing, I think it fair to refer to two other men of the rank and file who rendered signal service at all times and under very difficult conditions. They were Detective Jack Williams of the Bristol Constabulary and Detective Skelton of the Windsor Borough Police. There were, of course, many others, but as space does not permit of detail I hope, if this book is ever read by them, they will appreciate my opinion of all their splendid individual efforts in the area of Etaples.

CHAPTER NINE

AUGUST 1914

By Esmee Sartorius

Like so many others when war was declared, I applied at once to the St John Ambulance, to which I belonged, to know if there was any possibility of their making use of me, my only recommendation being three months' training in the London Hospital.

I was told that only trained nurses were wanted, and so gave up hope, but three days later the British Red Cross got an appeal for forty nurses to be sent out to Belgium; five St John Ambulance nurses (VADs later on) were being sent, and I was asked if I would go. I naturally accepted with alacrity, and 14 August found us in Brussels. Most of us were taken to the Hotel Métropole, where we were to await orders. As there was a big battle expected any day, we should all be badly wanted.

Next day some of the nurses were sent to hospitals outside Brussels, and others, including M., my cousin (who was a fully trained nurse), and myself, were given posts in the Royal Palace, which posts, however, we never filled, as the next thing we heard was that the Germans were outside the gates of Brussels, and all the allied wounded were to be evacuated to Antwerp.

We were then given the option of returning to England at once; some returned, but we, M and I amongst others, elected to remain, as we were told we were wanted outside Brussels.

At 3.00pm next day the Germans marched in; it was a soul-stirring sight, seeing these impassive and tired-looking troops marching in to what seemed like a deserted town, every door and window shuttered and barred, and not a civilian to be seen or a sound to be heard, save the steady tramping of the German troops, regiment after regiment, guns, cavalry, Uhlans with their fluttering pennons on their lances. One felt that thousands of Belgians were waiting and watching behind their shuttered doors and windows, with bated breath and terrible anxiety lest anyone or anything should cause a disturbance, and so bring down the punishment of the enemy. However, nothing happened, owing to the notices which had been posted up everywhere, and the wonderful influence of Burgo-master Max, who had implored everyone to be careful and to give no cause or excuse for trouble.

Brussels being an unfortified town, he had begged the people to help in a peaceful occupation. His words had the right effect and, after a time, doors and windows were opened, and cafés put their chairs and tables outside again, and the town gradually resumed its everyday life, but with a strong undercurrent of fear and consternation at the terrible feeling that the enemy was really in occupation, and Brussels under German rule.

Panics were easily started these days, and one sometimes met a crowd tearing down a street terror-stricken, crying that the French were outside the gates and a battle beginning, and one had to turn and run with the crowd till the panic was over.

We heard there were a number of wounded lying not far outside Brussels, and M and I tried to get a car to take us out there to pick them up, but the Germans would not allow a car outside the gates just then, so we took a tram as far as we could, then walked, but could find no trace of them.

On our return from a trip out beyond the gates we heard we had been applied for, M— and I, to go to Charlerio to join a matron and two nurses who had gone there a few days before. We were given ten minutes to get ready, and were very glad to leave the hotel (which by this time was full of German officers), and to feel we were at last wanted. As there had been no fighting in Brussels, there was very little need for nurses.

We were raced off in a car by the Belgian Red Cross, and dumped down late in the evening at one of the hospitals in Charleroi; but could find no trace of our compatriots, though we searched all the hospitals, nor could we get any news of them. The town was still burning, and most of the houses were shelled, and had gaping windows and large shell holes, and the streets were littered with broken glass and bits of furniture; but every house flew a white flag of some sort, which had been no help to them, as the Germans said they had been fired on.

It was now getting very late, and we were told nothing could be done till the morning, so we gratefully accepted the offer of one bed from a kindly Belgian. We spent a sleepless night. The guns sounded so close and shook the house, and it was with great relief we saw the day break, and we started once more on our search, this time with more success, as we heard they were at a hospital at Marcinelle, 5 miles out of Charleroi.

We trudged there, leaving our luggage to follow, and found the matron and nurses in a semi-equipped hospital, desperately busy, and worn out with all the wounded who had been brought in a few days before from the battlefields nearby. The German wounded, slight cases and dying, had all been evacuated the day before we arrived, and we took this as a good sign that the Allies were near, especially as we heard the guns so close, but this was not the case, as the fighting was in reality getting farther away.

We had plenty of work, though no fresh wounded. The hospital was originally intended for a civil hospital, but before it was finished the war broke out, and it had to be hastily equipped as a front line hospital, and in consequence was very badly supplied, and though we found beautiful electric appliances none of them were in working order, and all water had to be heated on a small stove, and many beds were without mattresses.

Our matron very soon left us to look up some other nurses in Brussels. She took the offer of a seat in a car going there and that was the last we saw of her. M— had been left in charge.

The wounded were all French, and we found them extremely nice to look after. They were most grateful for all we did, and were much amused at the amount of cleaning and washing required by the English nurses, those of them that were well enough.

We had many exciting incidents and thrilling moments, especially when the German guards came round, as we never knew what they might be coming for. It was sometimes a search for a deserter, or to see that none of our patients were escaping. We never knew that it might not be to march us off, as rumour had it that we should be sent to Germany.

Life was one continual series of shocks; strange noises made us think we were being shelled; the electric light going out one night made us vividly imagine we were going to be blown up. Many of these scares ended in laughter, the French-men ragging us for our *crises de nerfs*, but they did not quite like it themselves, lying helpless in bed.

We had a very busy time, but our patients were being gradually taken to concentration hospitals in Charleroi or to Germany as soon as they were fit to move, and we realised that our work before long would come to an end, and we began to wonder what was to become of us.

We had had no news for a long time, all means of communication having been stopped. We had no idea what had happened anywhere, or what the English nurses in and around Brussels were doing, so thought we must try and get news somehow from Brussels. We found a Belgian who had means of going there, and we asked him to put our case before the American Minister, who, we knew, had been asked to look after British interests. We wanted some money advanced on our cheques, as we had practically nothing left, and for help to return to Brussels or England.

The only answer we got to our appeal from the USA Legation was that we were on no account to go to Brussels; that they could give us no money, and that we were to ask the German Commandant in Charleroi to give us a pass to England or Maastricht via Germany.

This answer completely nonplussed us, as we did not want to advertise the fact that we were four English nurses alone in a hospital inside the German lines, especially as we had heard a rumour that some of the nurses who had been in and around Brussels and who were supposed to have been sent to England by the Germans were last heard of in Russia.

All these reports made us very unwilling to apply to the German Commandant for passes; so we decided to wait till our last wounded had been taken, hoping something might turn up.

Food was getting beautifully less and less, meat very occasional, and we lived for the most part on beans and potatoes and soup made of the same, flavoured with many fryings in the frying-pan. This, by the way, got me into severe trouble with the old cook, Mme. Gustave, because when I, on night duty, had to warm up our scanty meal, washed and scoured the frying-pan, I was told next day that I had completely ruined the soup and beans for ever, as we now would never get enough meat or onions to bring back the flavour of so many fryings. I never heard the end of that flavouring. The bread was black and sometimes so hard we couldn't eat it, and other times so doughy that when thrown at the wall it stuck. We very, very rarely, as a great treat, had a mouthful of white bread given us by some kindly Belgians.

By now our last man had been taken from us, and we felt that something must be done at once, so, much against our feelings, we bearded the German Commandant, who kept us waiting for a very long time, and we heard the orderly we had spoken to first, and who spoke English very well, telling the Commandant that we wanted passes to England via Germany or Maastricht. This he flatly refused, saying we must remain in Charleroi; nothing would move him, and so we returned crestfallen to Marcinelle.

Having now no work to do, we spent our days making definite plans to escape. Our only anxiety was to get away quickly before the Germans could get any inklings of our efforts. We had been cheerfully assured by the Belgians that, if they did get wind of them, we should undoubtedly be shot. This we were more than ready to believe, and many a time had visions of being lined up against the wall.

We managed at last to get a small sum of money lent us by our Belgian friends, and after many hours of talking we finally came to the conclusion that our best plan would be to accept the offer of a Belgian mine-owner, who offered us the use of his coal miners' ambulance to take us part of the way.

We were advised to leave in the dead of night, and we arranged to dine with our friends the following night, telling the concierge at the hospital, whom we did not trust, that we should be spending the night with them. This we did, taking only a string bag with tooth-brushes, etc., and dressed in mufti, with our Red Cross brassards sewn in the bottom of our skirts.

After a marvellous dinner to speed us on our way, the ambulance picked us up at 2.00am. Two Belgian women accompanied us, as it was thought safer to go in a party. We had many nerve-wracking moments when we met sentries and guards, especially crossing the bridge out of Charleroi, the driver explaining that we were a miners' ambulance; after a few words he passed us on. In the early morning we arrived at Fleurus, where we took the tram to Namur, and where we arrived in a snowstorm, and then on to Liége, partly trams, partly trudging. These last two towns, as well as villages along the route, were in ruins.

We had palpitating moments when the sentries on the trains asked for our papers; all we had were 'laisser-passer' as far as Liége, which our friends had somehow managed to wangle out of the Germans, stating we were Belgians going to see sick relations. These we showed, but fortunately we struck men who could not read French, but we murmured something which seemed to satisfy them. Before starting on our journey we had agreed that M— and I would do the talking, as the other two nurses did not speak French, and we naturally did not want it known we were English.

We spent the night at Liége, a room having been found for us, starting off the next morning early, feeling we had the most difficult part of the journey before us with the frontier to pass. We were thrust into a market cart going to Maastricht with vegetables. All this had been arranged for us by our Macinelle friends, who had found out that Liége market-women carried on a trade taking refugees over the border.

Just before arriving at the frontier the owner of the cart said she could only risk three across, so that the other three must manage as best they could. A Belgian, one nurse and myself got out, and the cart drove on with the others. We walked a bit, then started to cross a field, and had just crawled under some barbed wire, and were beginning to feel we had escaped, as we thought it was the frontier, when to our horror, a loud voice called on us to halt, and we looked round and found a sentry covering us with his rifle. So we turned back, as we knew that if any of us tried to run for it one of us would, at least, be shot. The sentry then asked for our papers. This was a blow, as they only allowed us to Liége, and here we were well on the way to Maastricht. However, the man seemed only to worry about the German stamp, and, seeing that, told us we must go back to the road and in through the proper *douane*. This we knew we could never do. There wasn't a hope of our being allowed through, but we walked in that direction, and farther on tried again to cross, where we came on another sentry. This time we did not try to pass him, but came back again to the road, making up our minds as we walked on to bluff the next one if we met with one.

We did meet with one and he was busy with a young Belgian who wanted to cross, so we hurriedly pushed our German stamp out for him to see and pressed some money into his hand and walked away as unconcernedly as we could, and again crawled under the barbed wire, expecting any moment that we might be shot at. However, this time we were safely across, but to our horror another sentry appeared, only he turned out to be a Dutchman who laughed at our scared faces.

By this time we were almost without feeling one way or another; the strain since leaving Macinelle had been so great as we were always terrified that our escape had been discovered, and that we might be arrested at any moment.

We stumbled on to the market place at Maastricht, where we found the others, who had got safely over.

We had no sooner found rooms in a hotel when a message was brought to us from a man who wished to see us, and it turned out that he was an Englishman over there on military business, and wanted some very important papers taken to a certain Government office in London. We were not too keen about it, but eventually agreed to take them.

The next day we took train to Flushing, and after some difficulty, owing to our having no papers on us, and only our Red Cross brassards stamped with the German stamps in Brussels, we got passages across to Folkestone, where the authorities found it difficult to believe our story, and where we were detained till they had made enquiries at the British Red Cross headquarters in London.

So this was the last of our troubles, and we were thankful to be back once more in England.

Our reward came in the shape of the Mons Star.

CHAPTER TEN

THE LAST STAND OF THE BELGIANS

By Sir Philip Gibbs

During the first two and a half months of the war I was a wanderer in France, covering many hundreds of miles in zig-zag journeys between Nancy and the west coast, always on the move, backwards and forwards, between the lines of the French and British armies, and watching with a tireless though somewhat haggard interest the drama of a great people engaged in a life-and-death struggle against the most formidable army in the world. I had been in the midst of populations in flight, armies in retreat, and tremendous movements of troops hurled forward to new points of strategical importance. Now and again I had come in touch with the British army and had seen something of the men who had fought their way down from Mons to Meaux, but for the most part my experience had been with the French, and it was the spirit of France which I had done my best to interpret to the English people.

Now I was to see war, more closely and intimately than before, in another nation; and I stood with homage in my heart before the spirit of Belgium and that heroic people who, when I came upon them, had lost all but the last patch of territory, but still fought, almost alone, a tenacious, bloody and unending battle against the Power which had laid low their cities, mangled their ancient beauties, and changed their little land of peaceful industry into a muck-heap of slaughter and destruction.

Even in France I had this vision of the ruin of a nation, and saw its victims scattered. Since that day when I came upon the first train-load of Belgian soldiers near Calais, weary or lame dogs after their retreat, I had seen an interminable procession of fugitives from that stricken country and heard from them the tale of Alost, Louvain, Termonde, and other towns where only horror dwelt above incinerated stones, and scraps of human flesh. The fall of Antwerp resounded into France, and its surrender, after words of false hope that it would never fall, shook the soul of the French people with a great dismay. It was idle to disguise the importance of this German victory at the time when France, with every nerve strained and with England by her side, could hardly stem back the tide of those overflowing armies which had been thrust across the Marne, but now pressed westwards towards Calais with a smashing strength. The capture of Antwerp would liberate large numbers of the enemy's best troops. Already, within a day of this disaster to the Allied armies, squadrons of German cavalry swept across the frontiers into France, forcing their way rapidly through Lille and Armentèires towards Béthune and La Bassé, cutting lines which had already been cut and then repaired, and striking terror into French villages which had so far escaped from these hussars of death. As a journalist, thwarted at every turn by the increasing severity of military orders for correspondent catching, the truth was not to be told at any cost. I had suspected the doom of Antwerp some days before its fate was sealed, and I struck northwards to get as near as possible to the Belgian frontier. The nearest I could get was Dunkirk, and I came in time to see amazing scenes in that port of France. They were scenes which, even now as I write months afterwards, stir me with pity and bring back to my imagination an immense tragedy of history.

II

The town of Dunkirk, from which I went out to many adventures in the heart of war, so that for me it will always hold a great memory, was on that day in October a place of wild chaos, filled with the murmur of enormous crowds, and with the steady tramp of innumerable feet which beat out a tragic march. Those weary footsteps thumping the pavements an the cobble-stones, made a noise like the surging of waves on a pebble beach – a queer, muffled, shuffling sound, with a rhythm in it which stupefied one's senses if one listened to it long. I think something of this agony of a people in flight passed into my own body and brain that day. Some sickness of the soul took possession of me, so that I felt faint and overcome by black dejection. There was a physical evil amongst those vast crowds of Belgians who had come on foot, or in any kind of vehicle, down the big, straight roads which led to France, and now struggled down towards the docks, where thousands were encamped. From their weariness and inevitable dirtiness, from the sweat of their bodies, and the tears that had dried on their cheeks, from the dust and squalor of bedraggled clothes, there came to one's nostrils a sickening odour. It was the stench of a nation's agony. Poor people of despair. There was something obscene and hideous in your miserable condition. Standing among your women and children, and your old grandfathers and grandmothers, I was ashamed of looking with watchful and observant eyes. There were delicate ladies with their hats awry and their hair dishevelled, and their beautiful clothes bespattered and torn, so that they were like the drabs of the slums and stews. There were young girls who had been sheltered in convent schools, now submerged in the great crowd of fugitives, so utterly without the comforts of life that the common decencies of civilization could not be regarded, but gave way to the unconcealed necessities of human nature. Peasant women, squatting on the dock-sides, fed their babies as they wept over them and wailed like stricken creatures. Children with scared eyes, as though they had been left alone in the horror of darkness, searched piteously for parents who had been separated from them in the struggle for a train or in the surgings of the crowds. Young fathers of families shouted hoarsely for women who could not be found. Old women, with shaking heads and trembling hands, raised shrill voices in the vain hope that they might hear an answering call from sons or daughters. Like people who had escaped from an earthquake to some seashore where, by chance, a boat might come for them all, these Belgian families struggled to the port of Dunkirk and waited desperately for rescue. They were in a worse plight than shipwrecked people, for no ship of good hope could take them home again. Behind them the country lay in dust and flames, with hostile armies encamped among the ruins of their towns.

For a little while I left these crowds and escaped to the quiet sanctuary of a restaurant in the centre of the town. I stood up from the table, upsetting a glass so that it broke at the stem. Outside the restaurant was the tramp of another multitude. But the rhythm of those feet was different from the noise I had heard all day. It was sharper and more marked. I guessed at once that many soldiers were passing by, and that upon striding to the door I should see another tragedy. From the doorway I watched an army in retreat. It was the army of Antwerp marching into Dunkirk. I took off my hat and watched with bared head.

They were but broken regiments, marching disorderly for the most part, yet here and there were little bodies of men keeping step, with shouldered rifles, in line, grim pride. The municipal guards came by, shoulder to shoulder, as on parade, but they were followed by long convoys of mounted men on stumbling horses, who came with heaps of disorderly salvage piled on to dusty wagons. Saddles and bridles and bits, the uniforms of many regiments flung out hurriedly from barrack cupboards; rifles, swords and boots were heaped on to the beds of straw, and upon the top of them lay men exhausted to the point of death, so that their heads flopped and lolled as the carts came jolting through the streets. Armoured cars with mitrailleuses, motor cars slashed and plugged by German bullets, forage carts and ambulances, struggled by in a tide of traffic between bodies of foot-soldiers slouching along without any pride, but dazed with weariness. Their uniforms were powdered with the dust of the roads, their faces were blanched and haggard for lack of food and sleep. Some of them had a delirious look and they stared about them with rolling eyes in which there was a gleam of madness. Many of these men were wounded, and spattered with their blood. Their bandages were stained with scarlet splotches, and some of them were so weak that they left their ranks and sat in doorways or on the kerbstones, with their heads drooping sideways. Many another man, footsore and lame, trudged along on one boot and a bandaged sock, with the other boot slung to his rifle barrel.

Riding alone between two patrols of mounted men was a small boy on a high horse. He was a fair-haired lad of twelve or so, in a Belgian uniform, with a tasselled cap over one ear, and as he passed, the Dunquerquoises clapped hands and called out: 'Bravo! Bravo!' He took the ovation with a grin and held his head high.

The cafés in this part of France were crowded with Belgian officers of all grades. I had never seen so many generals together or such a medley of uniforms. They saluted each other solemnly, and there were emotional greetings between friends and brothers who had not seen each other after weeks of fighting in different parts of the lines, in this city across the border. Most of the officers were fine, sturdy young fellows of stouter physique than the French among whom I had been roving. But others had the student look and stared mournfully from gold-rimmed spectacles. There were many middle-aged men among them who wore military uniforms, but without a soldier's ease or swagger. When Germany tore up 'that scrap of paper' which guaranteed the integrity of Belgium, every patriotic man there volunteered for the defence of his country and shouldered a rifle, though he had never fired a blank cartridge, and put on some kind of uniform, though he had never drilled in a barrack square. Lawyers and merchants, schoolmasters and poets, actors and singers, farmers and peasants, rushed to take up arms, and when the vanguards of the German army struck across the frontier they found themselves confronted not only by the small regular army of Belgium, but by the whole nation. Even the women helped to dig the trenches at Liége, and poured boiling water over Uhlans who came riding into Belgian villages. It was the rising of a whole people which led to so much ruthlessness and savage cruelty. The German generals were afraid of a nation of *franc-tireurs*, where every man or boy who could hold a gun shot at the sight of a pointed helmet. Those high officers to whom war is a science without any human emotion or pity in its rules, were determined to stamp out this irregular fighting by blood and fire, and 'frightfulness' became the order of the day. I have heard English officers uphold these methods and use the same excuse for all those massacres which has been put forward by the enemy themselves: 'War is war ... One cannot make war with rose-water ... The *franc-tireur* has to be shot at sight. A civil population using arms against an invading army must be taught a bloody lesson. If ever we get into Germany we may have to face the same trouble, so it is no use shouting words of horror.'

War is war, and hell is hell. Let us for the moment leave it at that, as I left it in the streets of Dunkirk, where the volunteer army of Belgians and their garrison troops had come in retreat after heroic resistance against overwhelming odds, in which their courage without science was no match for the greatest death machine in Europe, controlled by experts highly trained in the business of arms.

III

That night I went for a journey in a train of tragedy. I was glad to get into the train. Here, travelling through the clean air of a quiet night, I might forget for a little while the senseless cruelties of this war, and turn my eyes away from the suffering of individuals smashed by its monstrous injustice.

But the long train was packed tight with refugees. There was only room for me in the corridor if I kept my elbows close, tightly wedged against the door. Others tried to clamber in, implored piteously for a little space, when there was no space. The train jerked forward on uneasy brakes, leaving a crowd behind.

Turning my head and half my body round, I could see into two of the lighted carriages behind me, as I stood in the corridor. They were over-filled with various types of these Belgian people whom I had been watching all day – the fugitives of a ravaged country. For a little while in this French train they were out of the hurly-burly of their flight. For the first time since the shells burst over Antwerp they had a little quietude and rest.

I glanced at their faces as they sat back with their eyes closed. There was a young Belgian priest there, with a fair, clean-shaven face. He wore top boots splashed with mud, and only a silver cross at his breast showed his office. He had fallen asleep with a smile about his lips. But presently he awakened with a start, and suddenly there came into his eyes a look of indescribable horror ... He had remembered.

There was an old lady next to him. The light from the carriage lamp glinted upon her silver hair, and gave a Rembrandt touch to a fair old Flemish face. She was looking at the priest, and her lips moved as though in pity. Once or twice she glanced at her dirty hands, at her draggled dress, and then sighed, before bending her head and dozing into forgetfulness. A young Flemish mother cuddled close to a small boy with flaxen hair, whose blue eyes stared solemnly in front of him with an old man's gravity of vision. She touched the child's hair with her lips, pressed him closer, seemed eager to feel his living form, as though nothing mattered now that she had him safe.

On the opposite seat were two Belgian officers – an elderly man with a white moustache and grizzled eyebrows under his high *kepi*, and a young man in a tasselled forage cap, like a boy-student. They both sat in a limp, dejected way. There was defeat and despair in their attitude. It was only when the younger man shifted his right leg with a sudden grimace of pain that I saw he was wounded.

Here in these two carriages through which I could glimpse were a few souls holding in their memory all the sorrow and suffering of poor, stricken Belgium. Upon this long train were a thousand other men and women in the same plight and with the same grief.

Next to me in the corridor was a young man with a pale beard and moustache, and fine delicate features. He had an air of distinction, and his clothes suggested a man of some wealth and standing. I spoke to him, a few commonplace sentences, and found, as I had guessed, that he was a Belgian refugee.

'Where are you going?' I asked.

He smiled at me and shrugged his shoulders slightly.

'Anywhere. What does it matter? I have lost everything. One place is as good as another for a ruined man.'

He did not speak emotionally. There was no thrill of despair in his voice. It was as though he were telling me that he had lost his watch.

'That is my mother over there,' he said presently, glancing towards the old lady with the silver hair. 'Our house has been burnt by the Germans and all our property was destroyed. We have nothing left. May I have a light for this cigarette?' One young soldier explained the reasons for the Belgian debacle. They seemed convincing.

'I fought all the way from Liége to Antwerp. But it was always the same. When we killed one German, five appeared in his place. When we killed a hundred, a thousand followed. It was all no use. We had to retreat and retreat. That is demoralizing.'

'England is very kind to the refugees,' said another man. 'We shall never forget these things.'

The train stopped at wayside stations. Sometimes we got down to stamp our feet. Always there were crowds of Belgian refugees on the platforms –

shadowy figures in the darkness or silhouetted in the light of the station lamps. They were encamped there with their bundles and their babies.

On the railway lines were many trains, shunted into sidings. They belonged to the Belgian State Railways, and had been brought over the frontier away from German hands – hundreds of them. In their carriages little families of refugees had made their homes. They lived in them for some time after the War, hanging their washing from the windows, cooking their meals in these narrow rooms. They have settled down as though the rest of their lives is to be spent in a siding. We heard their voices, speaking Flemish, as our train passed on. One woman was singing her child to sleep with a sweet old lullaby. In my train there was singing also. A party of four young Frenchmen came in, forcing their way hilariously into a corridor which seemed packed to the last inch of space. I learnt the words of the refrain which they sang at every station:

A bas Guillaume!
C'est un filou
Il faut le pendre
Il faute le pendre
La corde à son cou!

The young Fleming with a pale beard and moustache smiled as he glanced at the Frenchmen.

'They have had better luck,' he said. 'We bore the first brunt.'

I left the train and the friends I had made. We parted with an '*Au revoir*' and a 'Good luck!' When I went down to the station the next morning I learnt that a train of refugees had been in collision at La Marquise, near Boulogne. Forty people had been killed and sixty injured. After their escape from the horrors of Antwerp, the people on this train of tragedy had been struck again by a blow from the clenched fist of fate.

CHAPTER ELEVEN

HOW TROOPER POTTS WON THE VC ON BURNT HILL

By Walter Wood

I saw a good deal of the Turks before we came to grips with them near Suvla Bay. I had gone out to Egypt with the Berkshire Yeomanry, and for about four months we were doing garrison work and escort work for Turks who had been captured in Gallipoli and the Dardanelles and sent as prisoners of war to Egypt. Our place was not far from Cairo. I was greatly struck by the size and physique of the Turks. There were some very fine big men amongst them – I should think the average height was close on 6 feet.

We had taken our horses out to Egypt with us, and all our work in that country was done with them; but as the weeks went by, and no call came to us for active service, we became disappointed, and got into the way of singing a song which the poet of the regiment had specially composed, and of which the finish of every verse was the line:

The men that nobody wants

meaning that there was no use for us as cavalry in the fighting area. But when the four months had gone, the order suddenly came for us to go to Gallipoli. By that time we had got acclimatised, a point we appreciated later, as the heat was intense and the flies were very troublesome.

From Alexandria we sailed in a transport, which occupied four days in reaching Gallipoli. Here we were transhipped to trawlers and barges, and immediately found ourselves in the thick of one of the most tremendous bombardments the world has ever known. Battleships were firing their big guns, which made a terrific noise, and there was other continual firing of every known sort. We were very lucky in our landing, because we escaped some of the heaviest of the gunfire. The Turks could see us, though we had no sight of them, and whenever a cluster of us was spotted, a shell came crashing over. Thus we had our baptism of fire at the very start.

We were in an extraordinarily difficult country, and whatever we needed in the way of food and drink we had to carry with us – even the water. Immense numbers of tins had been filled from the Nile and taken to Gallipoli in barges, and this was the water we used for drinking purposes, as well as water which was condensed from the sea, and kept in big tanks on the shore. Every drop of water we needed had to be fetched from the shore, and this work proved about the hardest and most dangerous of any we had to do after landing and taking up our position on a hill. Several of our chaps were knocked over in this water-fetching work.

While we were at this place we were employed in making roads from Suvla Bay to Anzac, and hard work it was, because the country was all rocks. We had landed light, without blankets or waterproofs, so that we felt the intense cold of the nights very much.

We had a week of this sort of thing, under fire all the time. I think it was on a Sunday we landed, and a week later we heard that we were to take part in the attack on Hill 70 or, as we called it, because of its appearance, Burnt Hill. There were immense quantities of a horrible sort of scrub on it, and a great deal of this stuff had been fired and charred by gunfire. I little knew then how close and long an acquaintance I was to make with the scrub on Hill 70.

It was about 5 o'clock in the evening when the great news came. We were to be ready at seven, and ready we were, glad to be in it. We did not know much, but we understood that we were to take our places in some reserve trenches. Night comes quickly in those regions, and when the day had gone we moved round to Anzac, marching along the roads which we had partially made. We reached Anzac at about 2 o'clock in the morning, in pitch darkness.

We had a pick and two shovels to four men, and took it in turn to carry them. Each man also carried 200 rounds of ammunition, so that we were pretty well laden. When we reached Anzac Cove we moved right in under the cliffs, which go sheer down to the sea; but there is practically no tide, so that the beach is safe. The only way to reach the shore was to go in single file down a narrow, twisting pathway.

We were on the beach till about 2 o'clock in the afternoon, when we were ordered to be ready with our packs, and we went up the cliffs, again in single file, forming up when we reached the top. Then we went a mile or so along the road we had marched over the night before – all part of the scheme of operations, I take it. Then we cut across to our right and saw a plain called Salt Lake, where we watched a division going into action under heavy shrapnel fire.

We were now in the thick of the awful country which I was to know so well. The surface was all sand and shrubs, and the great peculiarity of the shrubs was that they were very much like our holly trees at home, though the leaves were not so big, but far more prickly. These shrubs were about 3 feet high, and they were everywhere; but they did not provide any real cover. There were also immense numbers of long creepers and grass, and a lot of dust and dirt. The heat was fearful, so that you can easily understand how hard it was to get along when we were on the move. These obstacles proved disastrous to many of our chaps when they got into the zone of fire, for the shrapnel set the shrubs ablaze. This meant that many a line fellow who was hit during the fighting on Hill 70 fell among the burning furze and was burned to death where he lay.

As we were waiting for our turn, we could see the other chaps picking their way through this burning stuff, and charging on towards the Turkish trenches. When our own turn came, the scrub was burning less fiercely, and to some extent we were able to choose our way and avoid the blazing patches. We ran whenever we got the chance, making short rushes; but when we got into the real zone of fire, we never stopped until we were under the protection of Chocolate Hill.

For half an hour we rested at the foot of this hill. From our position we could not see the Turks, who were entrenched over the top; but their snipers were out and bothering us a good deal. It was impossible to see these snipers, because they hid themselves most cunningly in the bushes, and had their faces and rifles painted the same colour as the surrounding objects. However, we levelled up matters by sending out our own sniping parties.

We were on the move again as soon as we had got our breath back. We still understood, as we moved to the left of Chocolate Hill, that we were going to occupy reserve trenches. We went through a field of ripe wheat. About 2 yards in front of me was a mate of mine, Reginald West. I saw him struck in the thigh by a sniper's bullet, which went in as big as a pea, and came out the size of a 5-shilling piece. It was an explosive bullet, one of many that were used against us by the Turks, under their German masters. In a sense West was lucky, because when he was struck down he fell right on the edge of a dug-out, and I heard one of the men shout, 'Roll over, mate! Roll over! You'll drop right in here!' And he did.

The rest of us went on, though in the advance we lost a number of men. Some were killed outright; some were killed by shells and bullets after they had fallen wounded; and some had to lie where they had fallen and do the best they could. We pushed ahead till we struck Hill 70 again.

When we got to the reserve trenches I asked a chap how far away the Turks were, and he answered, 'About 1,000 yards,' but I don't think it was as much as that.

Now we began to ascend Hill 70 in short spurts, halting from time to time. We had fairly good cover, because the scrub was not on fire, though several parts had been burnt out. During one of these halts we were ordered to fix bayonets.

We had found shelter in a bit of a gully, and were pretty well mixed up with other regiments – the Borders, Dorsets, and so on. We first got the idea that we were going to charge from an officer near us; but he was knocked out – with a broken arm, I believe – before the charge came off. He was just giving us the wheeze about the coming charge when a bullet struck him.

How did the charge begin? Well, an officer shouted, as far as I can recollect, 'Come on, lads! We'll give 'em beans!' That is not exactly according to drill-books and regulations as I know them; but it was enough. It let the boys loose, and they simply leapt forward and went for the Turkish trenches. It was not to be my good fortune to get into them, however; in fact, I did not get very far after the order to charge was given.

I had gone perhaps 20 or 30 yards when I was knocked off my feet. I knew I was hit. I had a sort of burning sensation; but whether I was hit in the act of jumping, or whether I jumped because I was hit, I do not know. What I do know is that I went up in the air, came down again, and lay where I fell. I knew that I had been shot at the top of the left thigh, the bullet going clean through and just missing the artery and the groin by an eighth of an inch, as the doctor told me later.

Utterly helpless, I lay there for about three-quarters of an hour, while the boys rushed round me and scattered in the charge. This happened about a quarter of a mile from the top of the hill. I propped myself up on my arm and watched the boys charging.

I heard later, from a man who was with me in hospital at Malta – he had been struck deaf and dumb, for the time being, amongst other things – that the boys got into the Turkish third trench and that the Turks bolted. He told me that when they reached this third trench there were only seventeen Berkshire boys left to hold it. The enemy seemed to get wind of this; then it looked as if all the Turkish army was going for the seventeen, and they had no alternative but to clear out.

After the charge I saw this handful come back down the hill, quite close to where I was lying. I had fallen in a sort of little thicket, a cluster of the awful scrub which was like holly, but much worse. I was thankful for it, however, because it gave me a bit of shelter and hid me from view.

I had been lying there about half an hour when I heard a noise near me and saw that a poor, wounded chap, a trooper of the Berkshires, was crawling towards me. I recognised him as a fellow-townsman.

'Is that you, Andrews?' I asked.

He simply answered, 'Yes.' That was all he could get out.

'I'm jolly pleased you've come,' I said, and Andrews crawled as close as he could get, and we lay there, perfectly still, for about ten minutes. Andrews had been shot through the groin, a very dangerous wound, and he was suffering terribly and losing a great deal of blood.

We had been together for a few minutes when another trooper – a stranger to me – crawled up to our hiding-place. He had a wound in the leg. We were so cramped for space under the thicket that Andrews had to shift as best he could to make room for the newcomer. That simple act of mercy saved his life, for the stranger had not been with us more than ten minutes when a bullet went through both his legs and mortally wounded him. He kept on crying for water; but we had not a drop amongst the three of us, and could not do anything to quench his awful thirst.

That fearful afternoon passed slowly, with its grizzling heat and constant fighting, and the night came quickly. The night hours brought us neither comfort nor security, for a full moon shone, making the country-side as light as day. The cold was intense. The stranger was practically unconscious and kept moving about, which made our position worse, because every time he moved the Turks banged at us.

I was lying absolutely as flat as I could, with my face buried in the dirt, for the bullets were peppering the ground all around us, and one of them actually grazed my left ear – you can see the scar it has made, just over the top. This wound covered my face with blood. Was I scared or frightened? I can honestly say that I was not. I had got beyond that stage, and almost as a matter of course I calmly noted the details of everything that happened.

Throughout the whole of that unspeakable night this poor Bucks Hussar chap hung on. He kept muttering, 'Water! Water!' But we could not give him any. When the end came he simply lay down and died right away, and his dead body stayed with us, for we could neither get away nor move him.

During the whole of the next day we lay in our hiding-place, suffering indescribably. The sun, thirst, hunger, and our wounds all added to our pain. In our desperation we picked bits off the stalks of the shrubs and tried to suck them; but we got no relief in that way.

The whole of the day went somehow – with such slowness that it seemed as if it would never end. It was impossible to sleep – fighting was going on all the time, and the noise was terrific. We could not see anything of our boys, and we knew that it was impossible for any stretcher-bearers to get through to us, because we were a long way up the hill and no stretcher-bearers could venture out under such terrible fire.

Night came again at last, and Andrews and myself decided to shift, if it was humanly possible to do so, because it was certain death from thirst and hunger to remain where we were, even if we escaped from bullets. So I began to move away by crawling, and Andrews followed as best he could. I would crawl a little way and wait till Andrews, poor fellow, could crawl up to me again. We wriggled like snakes, absolutely flat on the ground and with our faces buried in the stifling dirt.

We managed to wriggle about 300 yards that night – as near as I can judge. Starting at about a quarter past six, as soon as the day was done, it was about three in the morning when we decided to rest, so that if we had really done 300 yards we had crawled at the rate of only 33 yards an hour!

A great number of rifles were lying about – weapons which had been cast aside in the charge, or had belonged to fallen soldiers; but most of them were quite out of working order, because they were clogged up with dust and dirt. I tried many of them, and at last found one that seemed to be in good working order, and to my joy I came across about fifty rounds of ammunition. Another serviceable rifle was found, so that Andrews and myself were filled with a new hope.

'We'll die like Britons, at any rate,' said Andrews. 'We'll give a good account of ourselves before we go!' And I agreed with him.

We were now some distance from the Turks, and I was terribly anxious to shoot at them; but Andrews was more cautious. 'If you fire they'll discover us, and we shall be done for,' he said. Then we shook hands fervently, because we both believed that this was the last of us, and I know that in thought we both went back to our very early days and offered up our silent prayers to God. We had managed to crawl to a bit of shelter which was given by some burnt-out scrub, and here we tried to snatch some sleep, for we were both worn out. We went to sleep, for the simple reason that we could not keep awake; but I suddenly awoke, because the cold was intense and I was nearly frozen. Luckily there were a lot of empty sandbags lying about, and I got two or three of these and put them on top of us; but they were really no protection from the bitter air.

When the morning came we made a move, and for the first time we were able to get some water; but only by taking the water-bottles from the poor chaps who had been knocked out.

Then we crept back to our shelter, finding immense relief from drinking the water we had got, though it was quite warm and was, I fancy, from the Nile.

We slept, or tried to sleep, there for the rest of that night, and stayed in the place till next morning. We must have been in what is called 'dead ground', a region which cannot be seen or touched by either side, and so it proved to be, for in the early morning there was a real battle, and the bullets were singing right over our heads.

'There's more lead flying about than there was yesterday,' said Andrews; and really some of the bullets were splashing quite close to us – within 6 feet, I think, though there were not many that came so near.

Andrews was bleeding terribly – every time he moved he bled; but I did the best I could for him with my iodine – I dressed him with mine, and he dressed me with his, and splendid stuff it is. Though we had nothing to eat we did not really feel hungry now – we were past the eating stage. I was very lucky in having four cigarettes and some matches, and I risked a smoke, the sweetest I ever had in my life.

Again we stuck the awful day through.

I was terribly anxious to move and get out of it all at any cost; but still Andrews was very cautious. 'No, we won't try till it gets dark,' he said. I felt that he was right, and so we waited, as patiently as we could, for the night. Some 3 or 4 yards from us was an inviting-looking bush, and we crawled towards it, thinking it would help us to get away and give us shelter; but at the end of our adventure we discovered that we had done no more than crawl to the bush, crawl round it, and get back to our original hiding-place; so we decided to give up the attempt to get away just then.

When the third night on the hill came we were fairly desperate, knowing that something would have to be done if we meant to live, and that certain death awaited us where we were. We had nothing to eat, and the only drink was the water, which was frightful stuff – I believe it was Nile water which had been brought. But though it was, we were thankful to have it. The water was warm, because of the heat, and was about the colour of wine.

We did not for a moment suppose that we should live to reach the British lines, which we believed to be not far away; but we risked everything on the effort, and in the moonlight we began to wriggle off. We had managed to get no more than half a dozen yards when Andrews had to give it up. I myself, though I was the stronger and better of the two, could scarcely crawl. Every movement was a torture and a misery, because of the thorns that stuck into us from the horrible scrub.

We had kept the sandbags, and with my help Andrews managed to get them over his arms and up to his shoulders. I fastened them with the pieces of string they have, and these gave him a good deal of protection, though the thorns got through and punished us cruelly. I was picking them out of my hands for three weeks afterwards.

Having crawled these half-dozen yards, we gave up the attempt altogether, and did not know what to do. We could see a cluster of trees not far away, about 100 yards, and there was one that looked fairly tall.

'If we can get to that tree,' said Andrews, 'I could lie there, if I had some water, and perhaps you could strike some of our chaps and bring help.' I had little hope from such an effort as that. Then Andrews unselfishly urged me to look after myself; but, of course, I would not dream of leaving him. I offered to carry him, and I tried, but I was far too weak.

What in the world was to be done? How were we to get out of this deadly place? There seemed no earthly hope of escape, when, literally, like an inspiration, we thought we saw a way out.

Just near us was an ordinary entrenching shovel, which had been dropped, or had belonged to some poor chap who had fallen – I can't say which, but there it was. I crawled up and got hold of it, and before we quite knew what was happening, Andrews was resting on it, and I was doing my best to drag him out of danger.

I cannot say whose idea this was, but it is quite likely that Andrews thought of it first. He sat on the shovel as best he could – he was not fastened to it – with his legs crossed, the wounded leg over the sound one, and he put his hands back and clasped my wrists as I sat on the ground behind and hauled away at the handle. Several times he came off, or the shovel fetched away, and I soon saw that it would be impossible to get him away in this fashion.

When we began to move the Turks opened fire on us; but I hardly cared now about the risk of being shot, and for the first time since I had been wounded I stood up and dragged desperately at the shovel, with Andrews on it. I managed to get over half a dozen yards, then I was forced to lie down and rest. Andrews needed a rest just as badly as I did, for he was utterly shaken and suffered greatly.

We started again at about a quarter-past six, as soon as the night came, and for more than three mortal hours we made this strange journey down the hillside; and at last, with real thankfulness, we reached the bottom and came to a bit of a wood. Sweet beyond expression it was to feel that I could walk upright, and that I was near the British lines. This knowledge came to me suddenly when there rang through the night the command: 'Halt!'

I obeyed – glorious it was to hear that challenge in my native tongue, after what we had gone through. Then this good English sentry said, 'Come up and be recognised!' not quite according to the regulation challenge, but good enough – and he had seen us quite clearly in the moonshine.

Up I went, and found myself face to face with the sentry, whose rifle was presented ready for use, and whose bayonet gleamed in the cold light.

'What are you doing?' said the sentry. 'Are you burying the dead?'

I saw that he was sentry over a trench, and I went to the top of it and leaned over the parapet and said, 'Can you give me a hand?'

'What's up?' said the sentry, who did not seem to realise what had actually happened – and how could he, in such a strange affair?

'I've got a chap out here wounded,' I told him, 'and I've dragged him down the hill on a shovel.'

The sentry seemed to understand like a flash. He walked up to the trench, and when I had made myself clear, three or four chaps bustled round and got a blanket, and I led them to the spot where I had left Andrews lying on the ground. We lifted him off the shovel, put him on the blanket, and carried him to the trench. These men were, I think, Inniskilling Fusiliers, and they did everything for us that human kindness could suggest. They gave me some rum and bully beef and biscuit, and it was about the most delightful meal I ever had in my life, because I was famishing and I was safe, with Andrews, after those dreadful hours on the hillside, which seemed as if they would never end.

When we had rested and pulled round a bit, we were put on stretchers and carried to the nearest dressing-station. Afterwards we were sent to Malta, where Andrews was for a long time in hospital.

The granting of the Victoria Cross for what I had done came as a complete surprise to me, because it never struck me that I had done more than any other British soldier would have done for a comrade.

I never lost heart during the time I was lying on Hill 70. All the old things came clearly up in my mind, and many an old prayer was uttered, Andrews joining in. We never lost hope that some way out of our peril would be found – and it seemed as if our prayers had been answered by giving us this inspiration of the shovel.

INDEX